MTTC©
Advantage

History (09)

Address all inquires to:

Kalmetrics
Kalamazoo, MI 49009
www.mttcadvantage.com
info@mttcadvantage.com

Disclaimer:

MTTC, the Michigan Test for Teacher Certification, and the MTTC logo are all trademarks of Pearson Education, Inc. or its affiliate(s). This publication is the property of Kalmetrics. It was not developed with, reviewed or endorsed by Pearson Education.

Printed in the United States of America.

ISBN: 978-0-9898096-1-0

Contents

Introduction

You've purchased—or are considering purchasing—this book for one reason, you need to ace the MTTC: History exam. You might have considered looking through notes from your American history, world history, and western civilizations courses, re-reading old textbooks, or maybe even purchasing additional textbooks to help you study. Begin this way and you'll see very quickly that there is just too much material to go through and too little time. After all, you're studying for a test that covers all of recorded (and unrecorded) human history! This test is the culminating pay-off from four (or more) years of undergraduate history, economics, political science, and geography courses. Moreover it's designed to challenge prospective history teachers, separating the professionals from the pretenders. Our point is that it is not an easy exam, however, like any test you can improve (sometimes drastically improve) your chances by practicing under realistic test conditions.

This is **exactly** what MTTC Advantage: History provides. This book is not designed to give you an overview of everything you might see on test day, clichéd pieces of advice on what to eat before the exam, or "secrets" you can use to fake your way through it. What you need is practical experience and a way to zero in on those areas of history that are your weakest. Our experienced team of professional historians and educators have worked to provide you with the highest quality exam simulations at the lowest possible price. The three practice exams contained in this volume are demanding. They will challenge you so that you will be prepared on test day.

Our exams are also the only ones on the market to-date that correspond to the new MTTC: History exam guidelines, effective October 1, 2013. If you need to prepare for the new MTTC: History exam, our practice test book is the only place to start!

We recommend taking each exam under realistic conditions. Write on the test book and limit yourself to the four-hour period you'll be provided on exam day. Check your answers after each test, identify areas of weakness and refine your study approach accordingly. If, for example, you are testing well on U.S. History Eras 1-6, show competency in the economics and political science sections, but struggle with World History Eras 3, 5, and 7, you will be able to narrow your focus and review materials related to those sections.

Study smarter, not harder!

The MTTC Advantage Team

Overview and Outline of the Exam

Questions for the MTTC History Exam are randomized (a question pertaining to the War of Jenkins' Ear might precede one about modern cartographic techniques) but are compiled according to the following distribution:

33%	**World History**
33%	**U.S. History**
27%	**Interdisciplinary Connections**
10%	**Historical Methodology**

33% World History

Questions here will test your knowledge of the entire scope of human history, from the earliest human societies (cir. 4000 BCE) to present day. Expect anything related to the social, political, economic, or cultural history of human kind. For your convince, and to help you identify areas of potential weakness, we've used the classifications for historical eras—the same standards used by the creators of the MTTC History exam—in the answer keys found at the back of this volume:

- Eras 1, 2, and 3: Early human society to 4000 BCE to 300 CE
- Era 4: 1000-300 CE
- Era 5: 300-1500 CE
- Era 6: 1400-1700 CE
- Era 7: 1700-1914 CE
- Era 8: 1900 to 1945 CE
- Era 9: World history since the Cold War

33% U.S. History

This is another broad category of questions. As with the world history section, questions here may be drawn from any area of U.S., or colonial American history and from America's social, cultural, economic, or political history. For your convince, and to help you identify areas of potential weakness, we've used the classifications for historical eras—the same standards used by the creators of the MTTC History exam—in the answer keys found at the back of this volume:

- Eras 1, 2, and 3: Prehistoric America to 1800 CE
- Era 4: 1792 to 1861 CE
- Era 5: 1850 to 1877 CE
- Era 6: 1870 to 1920 CE
- Era 7: 1920 to 1945 CE
- Era 8: 1945 to 1970 CE
- Era 9: 1970 to the present

· *A detailed outline of the MTTC History test objectives, with a more thorough breakdown of individual sections and historical eras is free to the public through the official MTTC website www.mttc.nesinc.com.*

24% "Interdisciplinary Perspectives"

Questions here might ask you for basic definitions or concepts from economics, political science, or geography, but might also ask you to think about how these areas affect (or are affected by) the professional study of history. For your convince, and to help you identify areas of potential weakness, we've used the classifications for historical eras—the same standards used by the creators of the MTTC History exam—in the answer keys found at the back of this volume:

- Geography, Physical Features and Concepts
- Relationship Between Geography and History
- Economics, Concepts and Relationship Between Economics and History
- Political Science, Concepts and Relationship Between Political Science and History
- Democratic Values, Citizenship, Public Policy

10% "Historical Concepts and Skills"

This includes the basic terms, definitions, and methods used by historians. Questions in this category are broadly conceived but may be contextualized in a specific historical era. The purpose is to see how well you understand what professional historians do, and why they do it.

Exam 1

Read the following passage excerpted from Christopher Columbus' letter to Raphael Sanchez to answer the three questions that follow.

Knowing that it will afford you pleasure to learn that I have brought my undertaking to a successful termination, I have decided upon writing you this letter to acquaint you with all the events which have occurred in my voyage, and the discoveries which have resulted from it. Thirty-three days after my departure from Cadiz' I reached the Indian sea, where I discovered many islands, thickly peopled, of which I took possession without resistance in the name of our most illustrious Monarch, by public proclamation and with unfurled banners.

The inhabitants of both sexes in this island, and in all the others which I have seen, or of which I have received information, go always naked as they were born, with the exception of some of the women, who use the covering of a leaf, or small bough, or an apron of cotton which they prepare for that purpose. None of them, as I have already said, are possessed of any iron, neither have they weapons, being unacquainted with, and indeed incompetent to use them, not from any deformity of body (for they are well-formed), but because they are timid and full of fear. They carry however in lieu of arms, canes dried in the sun, on the ends of which they fix heads of dried wood sharpened to a point, and even these they dare not use habitually; for it has often occurred when I have sent two or three of my men to any of the villages to speak with the natives, that they have come out in a disorderly troop, and have fled in such haste at the approach of our men, that the fathers forsook their children and the children their fathers.

This timidity did not arise from any loss or injury that they had received from us; for, on the contrary, I gave to all I approached whatever articles I had about me, such as cloth and many other things, taking nothing of theirs in return: but they are naturally timid and fearful. As soon however as they see that they are safe, and have laid aside all fear, they are very simple and honest, and exceedingly liberal with all they have; none of them refusing any thing he may possess when he is asked for it, but on the contrary inviting us to ask them. They exhibit great love towards all others in preference to themselves: they also give objects of great value for trifles, and content themselves with very little or nothing in return. I however forbad that these trines and articles of no value (such as pieces of dishes, plates, and glass, keys, and leather straps) should be given to them, although if they could obtain them, they imagined themselves to be possessed of the most beautiful trinkets in the world.

1. Which of the following best explains Columbus' attitude towards native peoples of the New World?

   A. Exploitative, natives are cowardly and should be ruled.

   B. Paternalistic, natives are like innocent children and need to be protective.

   C. Cautious, natives were so dissimilar from Europeans that Columbus did not know what his best course of action should be.

   D. Ambivalent, Columbus had no opinion of these people. His description is completely objective.

2. Why might Columbus feel it was important to include this description in his letter home?

   A. By describing the natives as cowardly and timid, Columbus thought others might consider opening up a slave trade in the West Indies.

   B. He was looking to finance more expeditions and wanted to show that there was no danger.

   C. This is nothing more than an attempt to add color to his descriptions of the New World.

   D. His intention was to imply that natives required Christianity and needed a strong monarchial authority.

3. Which of the following best represents Christopher Columbus' first impressions of native peoples of the New World?

   A. Indians were warlike savages bent on conquest.

   B. South American civilizations were technologically and intellectually superior to the disorganized cousins to the north.

   C. Christianity would work well among these innocent people.

   D. It would be impossible to rule such a diversity of native people; linguistic, cultural, and religious differences would impede any attempt.

Read the following extract from Martin Luther's Ninety-Five Thesis (1517) and answer the three questions that follow.

Spare me, most reverend Father in Christ, most illustrious Prince, if I, the very dregs of humanity, have dared to think of addressing a letter to the eminence of your sublimity. The Lord Jesus is my witness that, in the consciousness of my own pettiness and baseness, I have long put off the doing of that which I have now hardened my forehead to perform, moved thereto most especially by the sense of that faithful duty which I feel that I owe to your most reverend Fatherhood in Christ. May your Highness then in the meanwhile deign to cast your eyes upon one grain of dust, and, in your pontifical clemency, to understand my prayer.

Papal indulgences are being carried about, under your most distinguished authority, for the building of St. Peter's. In respect of these I do not so much accuse the extravagant sayings of the preachers, which I have not heard, but I grieve at the very false ideas which the people conceive from them, and which are spread abroad in common talk on every side—namely, that unhappy souls believe that, if they buy letters of indulgences, they are sure of their salvation; also, that, as soon as they have thrown their contribution into the chest, souls forthwith fly out of purgatory; and furthermore, that so great is the grace thus conferred, that there is no sin so great—even, as they say, if, by an impossibility, any one had violated the Mother of God—but that it may be pardoned; and again, that by these indulgences a man is freed from all punishment and guilt.

O gracious God! it is thus that the souls committed to your care, most excellent Father, are being taught unto their death, and a most severe account, which you will have to render for all of them, is growing and increasing. Hence I have not been able to keep silence any longer on this subject, for by no function of a bishop's office can a man become sure of salvation, since he does not even become sure through the grace of God infused into him, but the Apostle bids us to be ever working out our salvation in fear and trembling.

Why then, by these false stories and promises of pardon, do the preachers of them make the people to feel secure and without fear? Since indulgences confer absolutely no good on souls as regards salvation or holiness, but only take away the outward penalty which was wont of old to be canonically imposed. Lastly, works of piety and charity are infinitely better than indulgences, and yet they do not preach these with such display or so much zeal; nay, they keep silence about them for the sake of preaching pardons. And yet it is the first and sole duty of all bishops, that the people should learn the Gospel and Christian charity: for Christ nowhere commands that indulgences should be preached. What a dreadful thing it is, then, what peril to a bishop, if, while the Gospel is passed over in silence, he permits nothing but the noisy outcry of indulgences to be spread among his people, and bestows more care on these than on the Gospel! Will not Christ say to them: "Straining at a gnat, and swallowing a camel"?

4. What is the primary purpose of this document?

   A. To split off from the Catholic Church and form a new religious movement.

   B. Luther wanted priests to focus less on ideas that benefited only the Church in Rome.

   C. Luther is asking his parishioners to ignore the opulence and decadence of the Catholic Church and return to lives of poverty.

   D. To end the Catholic Church's involvement in indulgences.

5. Where does this work fit within the Protestant movement?

   A. This represents the first time anyone challenged the authority of a papal practice.

   B. The 95-Thesis called only for reforms within the church, not an absolute break.

   C. This launched the Huguenot movement.

   D. Luther's reforms helped initiate a Catholic reformation that swept through northern Europe for a time.

6. Which of the following best describes the tone of this work?

   A. Hostile and confrontational

   B. Academic and deferential.

   C. Argumentative and sarcastic.

   D. Zealous.

7. All of the following helped create the American baby boom of the 1950s, except:

A. Rising consumer confidence prompted by government spending

B. New social inhibitions against bachelorhood

C. Advances in medical science that included cures for tuberculosis and polio

D. Declines in the average age of marriage

8. In 732 Charles "the Hammer" Martel defeated a force of 80,000 Islamic invaders at the Battle of Tours. Why do historians consider this event significant?

A. It halted the northern advance of Islam; Christianity remained the predominant religion of Europe.

B. The battle marks the first appearance of gunpowder in Western civilization.

C. Most believe Martel's victory marks the official end of the Western Roman Empire.

D. Islamic warriors brought plague-carrying rats with them; the Battle of Tours is believed to have initiated the Black Plague in Europe.

9. How did the Cuban Middle Crisis affect U.S.-Soviet relations?

A. It increased tensions on either side and contributed to expanded nuclear arms testing

B. Tensions cooled somewhat. Peaceful gestures – including a direct line between the country's leaders – helped calm both sides

C. The first in a series of nuclear arms reduction treaties was help shortly after the conflict

D. The governments of both countries changed tactics and began seeking alternative, non-military means to undermine each other

Read the passages below concerning the nullification crisis and answer the two questions that follow.

Passage A

If those who administer the General Government be permitted to transgress the limits fixed by that compact, by a total disregard to the special delegations of power therein contained, an annihilation of the State Governments, and the erection upon their ruins of a general consolidated government will be the inevitable consequence. That the principle and construction contended for by sundry of the State Legislatures, that the general government is the exclusive judge of the extent of the powers delegated to it, stop nothing short of despotism, since the discretion of those who administer the Government, and not the Constitution, would be the measure of their powers. That the several States who formed that instrument, being sovereign and independent, have the unquestionable right to judge of its infraction, and that a nullification by those sovereignties, of all unauthorized acts done under color of that instrument, is rightful remedy.

Passage B

That New-England feels, at present, a deep interest in the Tariff is unquestionable-and how happens it? She found, many years since, the protecting principle admitted and acted upon by the General Government—South Carolina herself having led the way to its establishment. The South then complained of distress as they do now—they were not as prosperous as they wished—and, not seeing that the reason of their poverty was the possession of slaves, they sought relief in a protecting Tariff. New-England was, and, thank God, now is, free-unfettered—uncursed by a black population held to perpetual servitude—and, as a natural consequence, our capitalists vested a large portion of their funds in manufactures. Our establishments for the manufacture of domestic goods were the effect, not the cause of the Tariff. The faith of the government once pledged, and a large amount of property invested, it would be madness to repeal the protecting laws. Do the Southern gentry think that, after they themselves have procured the establishment of the principle of impost duties, and, by these means, induce us to embark our capital in a particular branch of industry, we shall look on tamely and complacently, whilst they are endeavoring to effect a nullification of their own acts and our consequent bankruptcy and ruin?

10. The argument of Passage A would be most enhanced by a reference to:

    A. The Kentucky and Virginia Resolutions.

    B. The First Amendment.

    C. The Tenth Amendment.

    D. The Declaration of Independence.

11. The author of Passage B links the argument for nullification directly to:

    A. Slavery

    B. Northern despotism

    C. Foreign influence

    D. The southern emphasis on manufacturing.

Use the following excerpt from Herbert Spencer's 1857 essay *Progress: Its Law and Cause* to answer the four questions that follow.

Whether an advance from the homogeneous to the heterogeneous is or is not displayed in the biological history of the globe, it is clearly enough displayed in the progress of the latest and most heterogeneous creature-Man. It is alike true that, during the period in which the Earth has been peopled, the human organism has become more heterogeneous among the civilized divisions of the species and that the species, as a whole, has been growing more heterogeneous in virtue of the multiplication of races and the differentiation of these races from each other.

While the governing part has been undergoing the complex development above described, the governed part has been undergoing an equally complex development, which has resulted in that minute division of labour characterizing advanced nations. It is needless to trace out this progress from its first stages, up through the caste divisions of the East and the incorporated guilds of Europe, to the elaborate producing and distributing organization existing among ourselves. Political economists have made familiar to all, the evolution which, beginning with a tribe whose members severally perform the same actions each for himself, ends with a civilized community whose members severally perform different actions for each other; and they have further explained the evolution through which the solitary producer of any one commodity, is transformed into a combination of producers who united under a master, take separate parts in the manufacture of such commodity.

But there are yet other and higher phases of this advance from the homogeneous to the heterogeneous in the industrial structure of the social organism. Long after considerable progress has been made in the division of labour among different classes of workers, there is still little or no division of labour among the widely separated parts of the community: the nation continues comparatively homogeneous in the respect that in each district the same occupations are pursued. But when roads and other means of transit become numerous and good, the different districts begin to assume different functions, and to become mutually dependent. The calico manufacture locates it self in this county, the woolen cloth manufacture in that; silks are produced here, lace there; stockings in one place, shoes in another; pottery, hardware, cutlery, come to have their special towns; and ultimately every locality becomes more or less distinguished from the rest by the leading occupation carried on in it. Nay, more, this subdivision of functions shows itself not only among the different parts of the same nation, but among different nations.

That exchange of commodities which free-trade promises so greatly to increase, will ultimately have the effect of specializing, in a greater or less degree, the industry of each people. So that beginning with a barbarous tribe, almost if not quite homogeneous in the functions of its members, the progress has been, and still is, towards an economic aggregation of the whole human race, growing ever more heterogeneous in respect of the separate functions assumed by separate nations, the separate functions assumed by the local sections of each nation, the separate functions assumed by the many kinds of makers and traders in each town, and the separate functions assumed by the workers united in producing each commodity.

12. Which of the following best explains the purpose behind this passage?

    A. The author intends to demonstrate the progression of human kind, from chaos and disorder to reason and harmony.

    B. The purpose is to show that individualism, in race, class, organization, and labor, is a natural and expected phenomenon.

    C. To explain the necessary forces of production in modern society.

    D. The author hopes to show how workers are entirely dissimilar from all other classes of people.

13. What larger historical movement does this excerpt point to?

    A. Fascism

    B. Colonialism

    C. Social Darwinism

    D. The Social Gospel

14. What conclusion might be reached after reading the above?

    A. The rights of workers were natural and should thus be protected by the government. When a government ignores these rights it foments rebellion.

    B. Over-specialization, as in the case of linen manufacturers, is problematic. It works against free-trade and will lead to higher prices.

    C. Human evolution trended toward individualism, government intervention in human affairs was thus counter productive.

    D. Casts and social divisions of any kind will always have a negative effect on government.

15. Which of the following best represents the author's assumption?

    A. Government bureaucracies are an inherent good.

    B. The masses should be given equal share in government.

    C. The American way of life needs to be protected at all costs.

    D. Society is evolving towards greater levels of individual freedom.

16. The "melting pot" of the United States is an example of the geographical concept known as:

  A. Regional interdependence.

  B. Cultural diffusion.

  C. Environmental flux.

  D. Human systems.

17. Unlike the Nile River to Egypt, the Yangtze River of China:

  A. Runs the entire length of the country

  B. Provides a natural political boundary

  C. Is susceptible to irregular flooding

  D. Flows South to North

18. Which of the following best describes the state of the American economy in the late 1970s?

  A. Rampant government spending and declining productivity led to a steep inflation curve and rising unemployment

  B. Deregulation of the financial service sector increased profits for private corporations but not average worker salaries

  C. A series of economic recessions forced the government to increase subsidies and financial assistance to the poor

  D. The Vietnam War created a brief economic boom that saw unemployment drop to all-time lows

19. John D. Rockefeller's system of horizontal integration allowed Standard Oil to:

  A. Lower the costs of production and price other companies out of the market

  B. Centralize operational control and regulate the entire process of production

  C. Purchase the stock of other companies and avoid charges of collusion and price fixing

  D. Distribute market share equally among his competitors

20. George H.W. Bush's bid for re-election sputtered because of:

  A. Cuts to Regan-era tax breaks

  B. Indecisive leadership in cold-war ear politics

  C. Failures to control the growth of Iraqi power in the Persian Gulf

  D. His administrations inability to broker a peace deal between Israel and Palestine

21. Which of the following best describes the religious practices of Shang period rulers?

A. Human sacrifice and divination, through oracle bones, allowed deceased ancestors to influence human affairs

B. As god-kings, Shang rulers did not pray or participate in the worship of other deities

C. Shang rulers were frequently buried alive in massive underground stone places. This was thought to ensure their immortality

D. Shang rulers invoked the "Mandate of Heaven", their rightful place as divinely sanctioned leaders, to justify their authority

22. Which of the following best describes the religion of the Roman Republic?

A. Personal, religious was not celebrated openly but considered intimate and inward looking.

B. Familial, Romans worshiped gods and goddesses but also the spirits of dead ancestors.

C. Highly structured, a system of priests, sub-priests, vestal virgins, and oracles gave religious practice a defined form.

D. Civic-minded, religion was meant to unite people with the community and provide a sense of civic duty.

23. Use the list below to answer the question that follows:

A bank panic and a political scandal involving Union Pacific railroad.

Violence and intimidation by southern whites.

The end of Republican-controlled state legislatures.

Declining interest among Northern politicians.

The withdrawl of federal troops.

The events listed above best describe which of the following?

A. Motivations behind the start of the Civil War.

B. Items for political debate in the mid-term elections of 1862.

C. Factors that helped to undermine popular support for Reconstruction.

D. Reasons behind the nullification crises.

24. Which of the following can be said of the modern city of Istanbul?

A. It was built on the remains of the Roman city of Nicea

B. It was once ruled by Mongolian war lords

C. It is situated between the contents of Asia and Europe

D. It was the one Mediterranean city untouched by the Roman Empire

25. The "Wilderness Road", a heavily traveled passage into the early American West, passed through the Appalachian Mountains by way of the:

A. Ohio Valley

B. Cumberland Gap

C. Ohio River

D. Green Mountain

26. Justice among the early Germanic peoples depended upon:

A. A written constitution.

B. The code of Hammurabi.

C. Private vengeance and blood feuds.

D. Astrological signs

Use the following excerpt from The French National Assembly's *Declaration of the Rights of Man and of the Citizen* (1789) to answer the three questions that follow.

The representatives of the French people, organized as a National Assembly, believing that the ignorance, neglect, or contempt of the rights of man are the sole cause of public calamities and of the corruption of governments, have determined to set forth in a solemn declaration the natural, inalienable, and sacred rights of man, in order that this declaration, being constantly before all the members of the social body, shall remind them continually of their rights and duties; in order that the acts of the legislative power, as well as those of the executive power, may be compared at any moment with the objects and purposes of all political institutions and may thus be more respected; and, lastly, in order that the grievances of the citizens, based hereafter upon simple and incontestable principles, shall tend to the maintenance of the constitution and redound to the happiness of all. Therefore the National Assembly recognizes and proclaims, thin the presence and under the auspices of the Supreme Being, the following rights of man and of the citizen"

1. Men are born into the world free and remain free and equal in rights.

2. The goal of all political association is the preservation of the natural and imprescriptible rights of man. These rights are liberty, property, security, and resistance to oppression.

3. No body or individual may exercise any authority which does not proceed directly from the nation.

4. Liberty consists in the freedom to do everything which injures no one else; hence the exercise of the natural rights of each man has no limits except those which assure to the other members of the society the enjoyment of the same rights.

7. No persona shall be accused, arrested, or imprisoned except in the cases and according to the forms prescribed by law. Anyone soliciting, transmitting, executing, or causing to be executed, any arbitrary order shall be punished. But any citizen summoned or arrested in virtue of the law shall submit without delay, as resistance constitutes an offense.

11. The free communication of ideas and opinions is one of the most precious of the rights of man. Every citizen may, accordingly, speak, write, and print with freedom, but shall be responsible for such abuses of this freedom as shall be defined by law.

12. The security of the rights of man and of the citizen requires public military forces. These forces are, therefore, established for the good of all and not for the personal advantage of those to whom they shall be entrusted.

27. What, according to this document, is the primary role of the French government?

A. To settle disputes, wage wars and collect taxes.

B. To protect the rights of French citizens.

C. The French government has no relevance under the arrangement described above.

D. The French King is the supreme lawgiver and subject to no one.

28. In what way is this document influenced by the philosophers of the Enlightenment?

A. There is an emphasis on the role of the military in civilian affairs.

B. A distinct separation of classes is the understood goal of government.

C. Individual freedoms and rights are understood to be natural and beyond the power of government.

D. The arrangement described is a plutocracy or, rule by society's wealthy elite.

29. Which of the following best describes the purpose of this document?

A. This was meant to curb the powers of the French King.

B. The poor (proletariat) were lobbying for rights in the aftermath of large-scale worker strikes.

C. By delineating the powers of the people, French citizens hoped to gain standing in the existing government.

D. It was meant to give organization and direction to the recent revolution.

30. While other law codes existed, the most famous is that of a Babylonian king who ruled around 1790 to 1750 BC in southern Mesopotamia. This code was very strict, regulated everything (family life, physicians fees), and demanded an "eye for an eye." It was known as the:

A. Corpus iuris civilis

B. Code of Hammurabi

C. Ur-Nammu law code

D. Salic Laws

31. Unlike Grover Cleveland, William McKinley:

A. Pressed Spain to reform its colonial policies in Cuba

B. Refused to acknowledge a native Cuban government

C. Asked the Spanish government to negotiate terms of independence with Cuban rebels

D. Pulled America into war with Spain despite widespread public resistance

32. Which of the following best describes the iconoclast controversies of the eighth century?

A. Iconoclasm was an effort to reunite Eastern (Greek) Orthodoxy with Western (Latin) Catholicism.

B. By destroying pictorial representations of Christ, the Mother of God, and saints, Rome's defeats could be avenged.

C. Iconoclasts, people who destroyed religious icons, were religious zealots, acting against the orders of the Roman Emperor.

D. Religious icons were directly tied to the corrupting influences of the Catholic Church.

33. What of the following factors was the most influential in bringing Americans into the Texas Territory in the 1820s?

A. The promise of free land and stories of goldmines, untamed horses, and natural wonders.

B. The Mexican Colonization Law offered affordable land prices and tax exemptions.

C. The popularity of Texas grew after the federal government designated it a slave state.

D. The U.S. government offered to pay settlers to relocate to Texas.

34. What allowed for the expansion Hitties in the second century BCE?

A. Their mastery of horse-drawn chariots and archery

B. Their ability to attract other into their culture

C. Advances in shipbuilding and navigation

D. A well-developed administrative hierarchy

35. The U.S. populist movement of the 1880s and 90s was initiated by:

A. Exploited farmers

B. Eastern bankers

C. Members of the Republican Party

D. Labor Unions

36. Use the list below to answer the question that follows:

> Theorized with the help of a "brain trust" of presidential advisors.
>
> The Civil Conservation Corps and the Works Progress Administration.
>
> New regulations placed on the number of hours worked by employees.
>
> Massive federal subsidies granted to farmers and loans to prevent farmers from going bankrupt.
>
> Attempts to restore the public's faith in banks.

The characteristics listed above are all elements of which of the following?

A. Progressive-era federal policy.

B. Depression-era federal policy.

C. Policies enacted under the Taft-Hartley Act.

D. Bills passed during World War II.

Use the passage below to answer the four questions that follow.

In my twentieth year, acting on my own judgment and at my own expense, I raised an army and used it to restore liberty to the commonwealth which had been oppressed by the tyranny of a faction. On account of this, the senate by laudatory decrees admitted me to its order and at the same time gave me consular rank in the expression of opinion, and gave me the imperium. It also voted that I as propraetor, together with the consuls, should see to it that the commonwealth suffered no harm. In the same year, moreover, when both consuls had perished in war, the people made me consul, and triumvir for organizing the commonwealth.

I undertook civil and foreign wars by land and sea throughout the whole world, and as victor I showed mercy to all surviving citizens. Foreign peoples, who could be pardoned with safety, I preferred to preserve rather than to destroy. About five hundred thousand Roman citizens took the military oath of allegiance to me. Of these I have settled in colonies or sent back to their municipalities, after the end of their terms of service, somewhat over three hundred thousand, and to all these I have given lands purchased by me, or money for farms, out of my own means. I have captured six hundred ships, besides those which were smaller than triremes.

Twice I have triumphed in the ovation, and three times in the curule triumph, and I have been twenty-one times saluted as imperator. After that, when the senate decreed dme many triumphs, I declined them. Likewise I often deposited the laurels in the Capitol in fulfillment of vows which I had also made in battle. On account of enterprises brought to a successful issue on land and sea by me, or by my lieutenants under my auspices, the senate fifty-five times decreed that there should be a thanksgiving to the immortal gods. Three times in my own name, and five times in that of my sons or grandsons, I have given gladiatorial exhibitions; in these exhibitions about ten thousand men have fought. Twice in my own name, and three times in that of my grandson, I have offered the people the spectacle of athletes gathered from all quarters. I have celebrated games four times in my own name, and twenty-three times in the turns of other magistrates.

37. To what historical era does the above belong?

A. The Roman Principate

B. The Roman Dominate

C. The Roman Kingdom

D. The Roman Republic

38. What is the author's primary objective?

A. The author seeks to aggrandize their part in the building of Roman prosperity.

B. The author is explaining how they came to hold legitimate power.

C. The author seeks to gain more military honors for past victories.

D. This message is intended for the public and is meant to incite public support for a struggle against corrupt politicians.

39. Which of the following would be the best historical use of the above?

A. To build a social history of early Roman people.

B. To construct a cultural history of race in the classical world.

C. As part of a political history of early Rome.

D. As an addition to a military history of Rome.

40. What historical event did the above most directly contribute to?

A. The fall of the Roman Republic

B. The fall of the Roman Empire

C. The barbarian invasions of the third century

D. The Roman social wars.

Use the following excerpt from William Graham Sumner's 1894 essay "The Absurd Attempt to Make the World Over" to answer the questions that follow.

It is repeated until it has become a commonplace which people are afraid to question, that there is some social danger in the possession of large amounts of wealth by individuals. I ask, Why? I heard a lecture two years ago by a man who holds perhaps the first chair of political economy in the world. He said, among other things, that there was great danger in our day from great accumulations; that this danger ought to be met by taxation, and he referred to the fortune of the Rothschilds and to the great fortunes made in America to prove his point. He omitted, however, to state in what the danger consisted or to specify what harm has ever been done by the Rothschild fortunes or by the great fortunes accumulated in America. It seemed to me that the assertions he was making, and the measures he was recommending, ex-cathedra, were very serious to be thrown out so recklessly.

Great figures are set out as to the magnitude of certain fortunes and the proportionate amount of the national wealth held by a fraction of the population, and eloquent exclamation points are set against them. If the figures were beyond criticism, what would they prove? Where is the rich man who is oppressing anybody? If there was one, the newspapers would ring with it. The facts about the accumulation of wealth do not constitute a plutocracy, as I will show below. Wealth, in itself considered, is only power, like steam, or electricity, or knowledge. The question of its good or ill turns on the question how it will be used. To prove any harm in aggregations of wealth it must be shown that great wealth is, as a rule, in the ordinary course of social affairs, put to a mischievous use. This cannot be shown beyond the very slightest degree, if at all.

The greatest question of all about American democracy is whether it is a cause or a consequence. It is popularly assumed to be a cause, and we ascribe to its beneficent action all the political vitality, all the easiness of social relations, all the industrial activity and enterprise which we experience and which we value and enjoy. I submit, however, that, on a more thorough examination of the matter, we shall find that democracy is a consequence. There are economic and sociological causes for our political vitality and vigor, for the ease and elasticity of our social relations, and for our industrial power and success. Those causes have also produced democracy, given it success, and have made its faults and errors innocuous.

41. What historical period does this work correspond to?

    A. The Antebellum Era

    B. The Gilded Age

    C. The Early Republic

    D. The Era of Good Feelings

42. Which of the following best represents the author's main point?

    A. The accumulation of wealth by "Great figures" is not wrong.

    B. Democracy is the best choice for a free society.

    C. The redistribution of accumulated wealth will help the economy move forward.

    D. European powers fear the growth of American business.

43. What is the relationship between American democracy and the accumulation of wealth?

    A. There is no relationship, both are mutually exclusive.

    B. Wealth relies on the stability of democracy.

    C. Democracy owes its very existence to the monetary systems in place.

    D. Politicians who argue against accumulated wealth show just how fragile American democracy is.

44. A geographer seeking to explain changes in rates of economic output and consumption over the long-term would be best served by referring to this concept:

A. Malthusian checks

B. Linguistic drift

C. Accessibility

D. Demographic cycle

45. What prohibited a quick victory in the Peloponnesian War (431-404 BCE)?

A. Athenian long walls protected their city while Spartan land armies remained impervious to Athenian sea power

B. Long periods of peace disrupted any significant loss of life on either side

C. Neither city-state had interest in the war, fighting was mostly restricted to small skirmishes

D. Religious observances limited the extent to which either side could actually engage in combat

46. Which of the following best describes the result of the so-called "Scopes Monkey trial"?

A. The immediate end to state laws prohibiting the teaching of evolution

B. The effective end of Christian fundamentalism in America

C. Scientific reason won a symbolic victory over Christian fundamentalism

D. States rights were reaffirmed by the court's decision to support the Tennessee law

47. In response to the Soviet invasion of Afghanistan, U.S. President Jimmy Carter:

A. Called for a military blockade at the Sea of Marmara

B. Ended grain shipments to the Soviet Union

C. Asked to resume the SALT II negotiations

D. Pressed congress for a declaration of war

48. Use the list below to answer the question that follows:

Cultivation of crops
Animal husbandry
Pottery
Textiles
Sophisticated tools

The traits listed above best describe which of the following eras of human existence?

A. Paleolithic Age

B. Bronze Age

C. Old Stone Age

D. New Stone Age

49. Napoleon's failure to conquer Russia was largely due to which climatologically phenomenon?

A. Torrential rains that turned roads to mud

B. The excessive heat of the Russian summer

C. A particularly harsh Russian winter

D. The rocky and mountainous terrain of the Russian steppe

50. Which of the following best explains Arthur Laffer's theory of supply-side economics?

A. Social entitlement programs, such as social security, cripple the economy and promote inflation.

B. Reducing the tax rate of the wealthiest citizens will stimulate the economy and provide job growth.

C. Increasing foreign exports is the best way to offset inflation

D. The supply of jobs is inversely proportional to the Gross Domestic Product (GDP)

51. Which of the following best explains the end of the Egyptian "Old Kingdom"?

A. Raids by Hittite warriors destroyed grain supplies which led to mass starvation.

B. Foreign rulers slowly worked their way into power end to the authority of the Pharaoh

C. The so-called "warrior pharoahs" led a series of disaterous military campaigns against kingdoms of upper Egypt

D. Pyramid building and prolonged drought weakened the Pharaoh and led to the rise of provincial authorities

52. In Germany, the early 1920s saw a period of:

A. Rapid economic growth prompted by rebuilding campaigns

B. Hyperinflation, steep declines in the value of the German Mark

C. Sustained militarism sponsored by the German Kaiser

D. Rabid intellectualism, most schools and universities were closed

53. Unlike civil law systems, common law:

A. Is based on a body of recorded laws

B. Has its origins in the precedent created by judicial rulings

C. Does not recognize a tiered structure of appeals courts

D. Uses statutes rather than customs and precedent

Use the excerpt below from Confederate President Jefferson Davis's inaugural address (February, 1861) to answer the two questions that follow.

The declared purpose of the compact of the union from which we have withdrawn was "to establish justice, insure domestic tranquility, provide for the common defense, promote the general welfare, and secure the blessings of liberty to ourselves and our posterity;" and when in the judgment of the sovereign States now composing this Confederacy it has been perverted from the purposes for which it was ordained, and ceased to answer the ends for which it was established, a peaceful appeal to the ballot-box, declared, that so far as they were concerned, the government created by that compact should cease to exist.

In this they merely asserted the right which the Declaration of Independence of 1776 defined to be inalienable. Of the time and occasion of this exercise they, as sovereigns, were the final judges, each for itself. The impartial, enlightened verdict of mankind will vindicate the rectitude of our conduct; and He, who knows the hearts of men, will judge of the sincerity with which we labored to preserve the government of our fathers in its spirit.

54. Which of the following best describes Davis's defense of Southern succession?

A. The South has a historic right to, and patriotic responsibility to protect, free and independent governance.

B. The peaceful, yet resilient qualities of the Southern states have been encroached upon by aggressive, war-like Northerners

C. White Southerners have been effectively disenfranchised by the Federal Government.

D. In order to be free, Southern states should unite behind a confederacy of like-minded allies.

55. What is the irony of Davis' invocation of the Declaration of Independence?

A. Personal liberty became an odd defense in a territory that defended the right to enslave people.

B. Taxation without representation was never part of the South's defense for succession.

C. Joining Southern states together into a "Confederacy" was contrary to the reason for its existence.

D. Davis' claimed Southerners were essentially disenfranchised by the North, this came at a time when only wealthy, land-owning Southern white Protestants could vote.

56. William Howard Taft, Charles Lindbergh, and other members of the "America First Committee" pressed for:

A. Pension benefits to former Army pilots

B. Protectionist tariffs that priced European goods out of the market

C. American isolationism and a policy of non-intervention in European wars

D. An aggressive policy of imperial expansion, starting with Latin America

57. Which of the following best describes the Chinese political philosophy known as "legalism"?

A. Nature's law compelled some to lead and others to follow

B. Humans are essentially good and will seek to do a good if placed in the right environment

C. Laws were the bedrock of all political power and contributed to the safety and stability of society

D. Absolute authority was the unquestioned right of divinely favored rulers

58. What did King William and the Normans bring to England in 1066?

A. The feudal system

B. Commerce and banking

C. Mercantilism

D. Spices and goods from the Far East

59. According to late-nineteenth century historian Frederick Jackson Turner:

A. Industrial production in the East pushed Americans westward and was ultimately the diving force behind democratic values

B. The frontier, now closed by white settlement, was the last artificial boundary between American regionalism and nationalism

C. America's democratic strengths were illusionary and the products of a mythologized "frontier type"

D. The settlement of America's western frontier allowed democratic values to thrive in a way not experienced by Europeans

60. All of the following were promoted by the Knights of Labor trade union, except:

A. Equal pay for women

B. A ban on child labor

C. An eight-hour workday

D. Better pay for Chinese immigrant workers

61. Which of the following most directly contributed to the rapid growth of American labor unions in the 1930's?

A. A series of government-supported union initiatives acts that made it easier to organize labor movement

B. Grass-roots efforts of individual union leasers and a growing number of successful union-sponsored strikes

C. The separation of the American Federation of Labor (AFL) from the Congress of Industrial Organization (CIO)

D. The inclusion of vast numbers of women and African-Americans into established unions

62. All of the following were aspects of the Southern plantation economy in the antebellum South, except:

A. A focus on cash crops, tobacco, cotton, and rice

B. Expanding demand from British manufacturers for raw materials

C. Rapid growth facilitated by new agricultural techniques and inventions

D. Decreasing connections with Northern banks and Southern manufacturers

63. The coordinates 46.0000° N, 2.0000° E represent which fundamental geographic theme?

A. Place

B. Region

C. Location

D. Relative place

Use the excerpt from Horace Mann's *Lecture on Education* (1840) to answer the two questions that follow.

No just judge will ever decide upon the moral responsibility of an individual, without first ascertaining what kind of parents he had; — nor will any just historian ever decide upon the honor or the infamy of a people, without placing the character of its ancestors in the judgment-balance. If the system of national instruction, devised and commenced by Charlemagne, had been continued, it would have changed the history of the French people. Such an event as the French Revolution never would have happened with free schools; any more than the American Revolution would have happened without them. The mobs, the riots, the burnings, the lynchings, perpetrated by the men of the present day, are perpetrated, because of their vicious or defective education, when children. We see, and feel, the havoc and the ravage of their tiger-passions, now, when they are full grown; but it was years ago that they were whelped and suckled. And so, too, if we are derelict from our duty, in this matter, our children, in their turn, will suffer. If we permit the vulture's eggs to be incubated and hatched, it will then be too late to take care of the lambs.

64. Which of the following best describes the intentions of the author?

A. To call for a national system of education.

B. He is arguing against the inclusion of females and minorities in public schools.

C. The focus is on the political damage schools can cause to governments.

D. The author intends to dissuade the public from seeking to educate their children.

65. To what does Mann link the French Revolution?

A. The laziness of the French people.

B. Their national system of education.

C. Their lack of a national system of education.

D. A natural ignorance of knowledge

66. Which of the following research hypotheses is best explored through the use of factor analysis?

A. A child's test scores across a wide spectrum of academic subjects may, when examined in the aggregate, speak to general levels of mental ability.

B. Popular culture intensifies the public's perception of and reactions to urban violence.

C. Health care in emerging countries is complicated by a culture of governmental mistrust and apprehension.

D. Tourism is often a catalyst for negative population growth in rural areas

67. The *Magna Carta* best illustrates which of the following principles of government authority?

A. Absolute monarchy.

B. Parliamentary rule.

C. Representative Democracy.

D. Constitutional law.

68. Which of the following best describes President Andrew Jackson's "spoils system"?

A. Jackson removed all political appointments from the previous administration and named his own.

B. Jackson pressed for the inclusion of foreign trade tariffs; all moneys collected were to be spent at the discretion of the federal government.

C. Jackson moved troops into South Carolina in an effort to move remove control from local farmers and prevent spoiling crops

D. This was simply Jackson's version of Henry Clay's "American system."

69. What did the French demand from America in the XYZ Affair?

A. New Orleans and exorbitant shipping duties from American merchants.

B. Bribes, "loans," and an official apology by the President.

C. A military alliance and the right to impress U.S. sailors when the situation arose.

D. Drastically reduced tariffs on goods imported to America.

Read the following excerpt adapted from Gengis Khan's letter to Ch'ang-ch'un (1219) to answer the three questions that follow.

Heaven has abandoned China owing to its haughtiness and extravagant luxury. But I, living in the northern wilderness, have not inordinate passions. I like simplicity and purity of manners. I hate luxury, and exercise moderation. I have only one coat and one food. I eat the same food and am dressed in the same tatters as my humble herdsmen. I consider the people my children, and take an interest in talented men as if they were my brothers. We always agree in our principles, and we are always united in mutual affection. At military exercises I am always in the front, and in time of battle am never behind. In the space of seven years I have succeeded in accomplishing a great work, and united the whole world in one empire. Heaven assists me to obtain the throne of the Chinese. It seems to me, that since the remote time such a vast empire has not been seen.

To cross a river we make boats and rudders. Likewise we invite sage men and choose out assistants for keeping the empire in good order. Since the time I came to the throne, I have always taken to heart the ruling of my people; but I could not find worthy men to occupy the highest offices. With respect to these circumstances I inquired, and heard that thou master hast penetrated the truth, and that thou walkest in the path of right. Deeply learned and much experienced, thou hast much explored the laws. But what shall I do? We are separated by mountains and plains of great extent, and I cannot meet thee. I can only descend from my throne and stand by the side. I have fasted and washed. I have ordered my adjutant Liu Chung-la to prepare an escort and a simple cart for thee. Do not be afraid of the terrific distance. Do not think of the extent of the sandy desert. Commisserate the people in the present situation of affairs, or have pity upon me and communicate to me the means of preserving life.

70. What is the purpose of Khan's letter?

A. Khan is writing to intimidate a rival ruler.

B. The letter is a simple boast, written only to promote Khan's claims to power.

C. He asks for a meeting with Ch'ang-ch'un who he hopes will offer political advice.

D. Khan needs financial assistance and is asking Ch'ang-ch'un for help.

71. What qualities does Khan claim to have?

A. He is a philosopher king with intelligence beyond normal men.

B. Khan is devoted to his religion and demonstrates his spiritual devotion.

C. Khan is a peaceful defender of Chinese values.

D. He is primarily a military leader who lives the spartan life of a solder.

72. What can this letter tell us about Khan's rule of conquered people?

A. He controlled his territories without regard to religious or political circumstances of indigenous populations.

B. He saw no place in his administration for foreigners.

C. He is a benevolent despot and desired to unify the people under one rule.

D. He hoped to overawe conquered people with shows of military force.

73. What effect did the Supreme Court case, "Brown v. Board of Education of Topeka (1950)" have an American Society?

A. It inspired similar reforms to immigration legislation

B. It helped bring about a series of civil rights reforms

C. It called for the creation of separate by equal schools in the south

D. It prohibited discrimination based on sex, national origin, or race

74. Which of the following best describes the apprenticeship system in early America?

A. It was limited to those who practiced trades or produced goods

B. The average length of apprenticeship was generally 1 to 2 years

C. Apprenticing masters were legally responsible for the health and education of individual apprentices

D. The system operated outside the law

75. Nathaniel Bacon's rebellion highlighted certain tensions within in colonial America; which of the following describes Bacon's lasting influence?

A. Nathaniel Bacon resorted to violence at a time when military power was maintained by social elites; his actions proved the illegitimacy of elite control.

B. The rebellion brought to light the powers inherent of a large and growing population of poor farmers and un-propertied commoners.

C. State militias exercised a quasi-independent status in the decades before the rebellion; Bacon showed that they were often subservient to the whims of landed aristocrats.

D. The violence of the rebellion, although not dramatic, gave the British monarch pause to consider the need to quarter troops to prevent further popular protests.

76. Use the following map to answer the question that follows:

The shaded areas represent the colonial possessions of:

A. The Spanish Empire

B. The French Empire

C. The British Empire

D. The Portuguese Empire

77. Which of the following best describes economic theory of John Maynard Keynes?

A. The "invisible hand" of the market determines the correct price of goods sold.

B. A flat tax on spending would, unlike our current graduated system, benefit the majority of Americans.

C. Low interest rates and increased spending promotes commercial growth and lowers unemployment.

D. Higher interest rates protect the economy from fiscally irresponsible decisions.

78. The medieval guild system provided a means to:

A. Participate in local government as guilds were often incorporated with existing bureaucracies

B. Regulate the quality of items produced

C. Encourage competition

D. Promote governmental policy

Use the following excerpt from the Gospel of Matthew (cir. 100 to 70 BCE) to answer the three questions that follow.

Seeing the multitude of people, Jesus went up the Hill. There He seated Himself, and when His disciples came to Him, He proceeded to teach them, and said:
"Blessed are the poor in spirit, for to them belongs the Kingdom of the Heavens.
"Blessed are the mourners, for they will be comforted.
"Blessed are the meek, for they as heirs will inherit the earth.
"Blessed are they who hunger and thirst for righteousness, for they will be completely satisfied.
"Blessed are the compassionate, for they will receive compassion.
"Blessed are the pure in heart, for they will see God.
"Blessed are the peacemakers, for it is they who will be recognized as sons of God. "Blessed are they who have borne persecution in the cause of righteousness, for to them belongs the Kingdom of Heaven.

You are the salt of the earth; but if salt has Light become tasteless, in what way can it regain its saltness? It is no longer good for anything but to be thrown away and trodden on by the passers by you are the light of the world; a town cannot be hid if built on a hill-top. Nor is a lamp lighted to be put under a bushel, but on the lampstand; and then it gives light to all in the house. Just so let your light shine before all men, in order that they may see your holy lives and may give glory to your Father who is in Heaven.

Do not for a moment suppose that I have come to abolish the Law or the Prophets: I have not come to abrogate them but to give them their completion. Solemnly I tell you that until heaven and earth pass away, not one iota or smallest detail will pass away from the Law until all has taken place. Whoever therefore breaks one of these least commandments and teaches others to break them, will be called the least in the Kingdom of the Heavens; but whoever practices them and teaches them, he will be acknowledged as great in the Kingdom of the Heavens. For I assure you that unless your righteousness greatly surpasses that of the Scribes and Pharisees, you will certainly not find entrance into the Kingdom of the Heavens.

You have heard that it was said to the ancients, "thou shall not commit murder, and whoever commits murder will be answerable to judgment." But I say to you that every one who becomes angry with his brother shall be answerable to judgement....If therefore when you are offering your gift upon the altar, you remember that your brother has a grievance against you, leave your gift there before the altar, and go and make friends with your brother first, and then return and proceed to offer your gift. Come to terms without delay with your opponent while you are yet with him on the way to the court; for fear he should obtain a judgement against you, and the magistrate should give you in custody to the officer and you be thrown into prison. I solemnly tell you that you will certainly not be released till you have paid the very last cent.

79. What can the above tell us about Jesus' ideas on living a good life?

A. Humility, honest, and charity are the qualities all should seek.

B. The wealthy are not able to pursue lives of peace and tranquility.

C. In order to maintain happiness we must seek the favor of our brothers.

D. The worship of God is all that is required for a good life.

80. Which of the following best explains Jesus' views of Hebrew law?

A. Hebraic law no longer existed.

B. Laws ceased to be the qualification for God's favor.

C. The laws of man were now seen as disruptive to the laws of God.

D. Laws existed but only as abstractions, they were not really to be followed.

81. How did these ideas differ from prevailing religious attitudes?

A. Roman authorities were no longer able to control the Christian self-determination.

B. Jewish leaders reacted by promoting a series of religious reforms.

C. Worship was no longer restricted to those with special understanding or access to places of worship.

D. A number of religious prophets were inspired to deliver similar messages of their own.

82. Which of the following is true of the Mercator projection map?

A. It is most inaccurate at the equator.

B. Distortion increases to infinity at the North and South Pole.

C. It is a development of the early 20th century.

D. It places the Atlantic Ocean at the center of the map.

83. What was one reason behind Italy's decision to abandon the Axis Powers alliance and join the side of the Allies in WWII?

A. The Allies promised Italy land in the event of an allied victory.

B. Germany continued to torpedo Italian merchant vessels despite repeated calls for ceasefire.

C. Austria-Hungry invaded Italian territory; the Italian government believed an alliance with the U.S. was the only way to save their sovereignty.

D. The Italian people desired monarchial authority; the Allies promised to return a king to the Italian throne.

84. Why did the British refuse to withdraw from the Northwest Territory at the conclusion of the Revolutionary War?

A. Communications between England and the western reaches of North America took months; the instructions British troops received also were confusing and not definitive.

B. The British were secretly planning to renew the war when the Americans least expected.

C. British officials argued that Americans were not meeting their debt obligations; they would abandon forts when and if Americans made good on their debts.

D. The British agreed to remain for the protection of Native Americans.

Read Abraham Lincoln's *Gettysburg Address* (1863) and answer the two questions that follow:

Fourscore and seven years ago, our fathers brought forth on this continent a new nation, conceived in liberty, and dedicated to the proposition that all men are created equal. Now we are engaged in a great civil war, testing whether that nation, or any nation so conceived and so dedicated, can long endure. We are met on a great battle field of that war. We have come to dedicate a portion of that field as a final resting-place for those who here gave their lives that that nation might live. It is altogether fitting and proper that we should do this.

But in a larger sense we cannot dedicate —we cannot consecrate— we cannot hallow—this ground. The brave men, living and dead, who struggled here, have consecrated it far above our poor power to add or detract. The world will little note nor long remember what we say here, but it can never forget what they did here. It is for us, the living, rather, to be dedicated here to the unfinished work which they who fought here have thus far so nobly advanced. It is rather for us to be here dedicated to the great task remaining before us — that from these honored dead we take increased devotion to that cause for which they gave the last full measure of devotion; that we here highly resolve that these dead shall not have died in vain; that this nation, under God, shall have a new birth of freedom; and that government of the people, by the people, for the people, shall not perish from the earth.

85. What document does Lincoln refer to at the start of his address?

A. The Declaration of Independence.

B. The U.S. Constitution.

C. The U.S. Bill of Rights.

D. The English Bill of Rights.

86. This document is most similar, in form and function, to:

A. Luther's *95 Thesis*

B. Augustus' *Res Gestae*

C. George Washington's first inaugural address.

D. Pericles' *Funeral Oration*

87. Studies related to new urbanism, gentrification, and redevelopment are terms most directly related to:

A. Physical geography

B. Physical systems theory

C. Cultural capital

D. Urban geography

88. The purpose of Alexander Hamilton's First Bank of the United States was to:

A. Allow for a decentralized, autonomous system of state financing

B. Regulate fiscal policy

C. Collect taxes and lend money to the federal government

D. Print currency

89. Which of the following best describes the value of neutral Border States during the American Civil War?

A. These states gave access to vital rivers, industrial centers, and manpower

B. Border States became increasing more southern in orientation as the war progressed

C. Areas within these states were rich in salt peter, ore, and other strategic resources

D. Confederate states saw these areas as important markets for slave labor, and capital

90. Which of the following best describes the immediate cause of the Great Depression?

A. A weak economy and a climate of speculative investment shook consumer confidence and led to bank failures and depressed consumer sales

B. Over regulation of free enterprise began to take its toll, businesses were less apt to expand and hire new workers

C. Deregulation of government securities raised the amount investors could buy on margin

D. Workers salaries quadrupled in the 1920s, leading to decreased profits and ultimately business failures

91. William Levitt is best remembered for his contributions to:

A. Mass production

B. Suburban housing

C. Electronics

D. Synthetic materials

92. A constitutional amendment guaranteeing "equality of rights under the law" regardless of sex was known as the:

A. Equal Employment Opportunity Act

B. Civil Rights Act

C. Equal Rights Amendment

D. Universal Declaration of Human Rights

93. Use the list below to answer the question that follows.

It began with the assassination of a foreign dignitary. Certain forces were aligned in the "Three Emperors League." The U.S. committed forces years after the conflict began. Conflict speeded a domestic revolution.

The characteristics listed above best describe which of the following conflicts?

A. World War I.

B. The War of Jenkins' Ear.

C. The French and Indian War.

D. The Philippine-American War.

94. Which of the following best describes The English Bill of Rights (1869)?

A. It reversed the conditions placed on the King of England by the Magna Carta

B. It established a tricameral legislation body

C. It reestablished the authority of the British Parliament

D. It put an end to the rule of the King of England

Use the following passage from Bede's *Eccleastical History of the English Peoples* to answer the three questions that follow.

I sent with much pleasure before this, O king, at your desire, the Ecclesiastical History of the nation of the Angles, which I had lately published, for you to read and judge of, and I now send it again to be transcribed and more fully studied, as you shall find time: and I delight greatly in the zeal of your sincerity, through which you not only earnestly I apply your ear to the hearing of the words of Holy Scripture, but also take diligent pains to become acquainted with the actions and words of illustrious men of former times, and especially of our nation. For if history relates good things concerning the good, the attentive hearer is excited to imitate that which is good; or if it reports evil things concerning the depraved, the religious and pious hearer is no whit the less incited, while he shuns that which is harmful and perverse, himself to follow more diligently the things which he knows are good and worthy of God. You also discerning by your great vigilance this very thing, are desirous that the aforesaid History should become more fully known to yourself, as well as to those whom Divine authority has appointed you to govern.

I humbly entreat the reader, that if anywhere in this that I have written he finds any things set down otherwise than as the truth is, he will not impute this to me, since, according to the true rule of history, I have simply aimed at committing to writing, for the instruction of posterity, such things as I collected from common report. Furthermore I humbly entreat all hearers or readers of our nation, to whom this same History may come, to remember often to intercede with the Divine mercy for my infirmities both of mind and body; and let them each in their respective provinces make me this return, as a remuneration on their part, that, since I have diligently taken care to set down, concerning the several provinces or the more important places, such things as I thought were worthy of mention and pleasing to the inhabitants, I may find among all of them the fruit of their pious intercession.

95. What effect did Bede intend his work to have?

   A. The intention was to give the English king a better understanding of his relm.

   B. Bede wanted to correct previous histories that reflected only the positive or favorable aspects of English history

   C. It was meant to unite the English people as one nation.

   D. He hoped to provide the English with a proper Christian heritage.

96. How does Bede expect readers to react to stories of "illustrious men"?

   A. They will serve as models they can learn from.

   B. Readers will be inspired to become "illustrious" themselves.

   C. The lives of these men, when read along with the Bible, is meant only to inspire the king.

   D. These lives show how God often intercedes in the affairs of humans.

97. Bede attempts to strike an unbiased tone here by:

   A. Claiming to speak only for a few of the English

   B. Arguing that all his information comes directly from the Holy Spirit.

   C. He says that he is just cataloging ideas that are common knowledge.

   D. A completely unbiased account is impossible and Bede recognizes this fact.

Read the following excerpt from "Federalist 15" by Alexander Hamilton and answer the three questions that follow.

It is a singular instance of the capriciousness of the human mind, that after all the admonitions we have had from experience on this head, there should still be found men who object to the new Constitution . . . .There is nothing absurd or impracticable in the idea of a league or alliance between independent nations for certain defined purposes precisely stated in a treaty regulating all the details of time, place, circumstance, and quantity; leaving nothing to future discretion; and depending for its execution on the good faith of the parties. Compacts of this kind exist among all civilized nations, subject to the usual vicissitudes of peace and war, of observance and non-observance, as the interests or passions of the contracting powers dictate.

If the particular States in this country are disposed to stand in a similar relation to each other, and to drop the project of a general discretionary superintendence, the scheme would indeed be pernicious, and would entail upon us all the mischiefs which have been enumerated under the first head; but it would have the merit of being, at least, consistent and practicable Abandoning all views towards a confederate government, this would bring us to a simple alliance offensive and defensive; and would place us in a situation to be alternate friends and enemies of each other, as our mutual jealousies and rivalries, nourished by the intrigues of foreign nations, should prescribe to us.
But if we are unwilling to be placed in this perilous situation; if we still will adhere to the design of a national government, or, which is the same thing, of a superintending power, under the direction of a common council, we must resolve to incorporate into our plan those ingredients which may be considered as forming the characteristic difference between a league and a government; we must extend the authority of the Union to the persons of the citizens, the only proper objects of government.

98. The author of this passage makes an appeal for:

A. Weak federal authority

B. Increased powers of the states

C. A strong central government

D. Diplomatic ties with foreign powers

99. Which of the following best explains the historical context of this excerpt?

A. This was written during the American Revolution.

B. It was part of the debate surrounding the ratification of the Constitution.

C. The views expressed were tied to the Hartford Convention (1815)

D. This was part of the debate over succession held in Virginia (cir. 1860).

100. According to the author, those who objected to the Constitution were:

A. Siding with the old powers of Continental Europe.

B. Anti-democratic.

C. At odds with the Confederation of states who hoped to ensure the peace and tranquility of the Republic.

D. Ignorant of the jealousies and foreign intrigues in America.

Exam 2

1. Throughout the Early Modern period (roughly 1350-1715), Italy was made up of a number of despotically ruled:

   A. Kingdoms

   B. Principalities

   C. City-states

   D. Duchies

2. Use the list below to answer the question that follows:

Most members did not wish to separate from the Church of England.
Desired to reform Christianity according to a simplified theology.
Persecuted by King James I.
Deeply influenced by the religious reforms sweeping through much of Europe.
Criticized "popish" liturgical rites.

The traits listed above best describe which of the following groups?

   A. The Puritans of the 16th and 17th centuries.

   B. Waldensians (otherwise known as Cathars).

   C. Reformed Catholics of England.

   D. Franciscan and Dominican monks.

3. The majority of U.S. Naval victories in the War of 1812 were on:

   A. The Atlantic Coast

   B. The Bearing Sea

   C. Lake Champlain

   D. The Great Lakes

4. Mental maps, the means by which we store geographic information and make sense of the world, are useful to understanding:

   A. Familiar landscapes.

   B. Spatial relationships between the familiar and the unfamiliar.

   C. How landscapes are formed.

   D. Migration patterns.

5. A map of the battlefield at Gettysburg is an example of a:

   A. Small-scale map.

   B. Large-scale map.

   C. Resource map.

   D. Political map.

Read the following excerpt from Jean-Jacques Rousseau's *Social Contract* (1762) and answer the three questions that follow.

Man is born free; and everywhere he is in chains. One thinks himself the master of others, and still remains a greater slave than they. How did this change come about? I do not know. What can make it legitimate? That question I think I can answer. If I took into account only force, and the effects derived from it, I should say: "As long as a people is compelled to obey, and obeys, it does well; as soon as it can shake off the yoke, and shakes it off, it does still better; for, regaining its liberty by the same right as took it away, either it is justified in resuming it, or there was no justification for those who took it away." But the social order is a sacred right which is the basis of all other rights. Nevertheless, this right does not come from nature, and must therefore be founded on conventions.

Laws are, properly speaking, only the conditions of civil association. The people being subject to the laws, ought to be their author: the conditions of the society ought to be regulated solely by those who come together to form it. But how are they to regulate them? Is it to be by common agreement, by a sudden inspiration? Has the body politic an organ to declare its will? Who can give it the foresight to formulate and announce its acts in advance? Or how is it to announce them in the hour of need? How can a blind multitude, which often does not know what it wills, because it rarely knows what is good for it, carry out for itself so great and difficult an enterprise as a system of legislation? The individuals see the good they reject; the public wills the good it does not see. All stand equally in need of guidance. The former must be compelled to bring their wills into conformity with their reason; the latter must be taught to know what it wills. If that is done, public enlightenment leads to the union of understanding and will in the social body: the parts are made to work exactly together, and the whole is raised to its highest power. This makes a legislator necessary.

6. Where do the people derive their authority?

   A. The monarch or ruling legislator give it to them.

   B. It natural to the human condition.

   C. Authority is taken by military force, not given or inherited.

   D. It is a sacred right.

7. The principals embedded here represent a larger philosophical movement known as:

   A. Humanism

   B. The Scientific Revolution

   C. The Renaissance

   D. The Enlightenment

8. Why are laws necessary?

   A. Laws unite the will of individuals with the larger public.

   B. Laws carry a moral imperative and are easily shared by all

   C. Laws provide equality because monarchs, supreme lawgivers, are bound by the same morality as others.

   D. Laws give voice to the individual concerns.

9. Which of the following best describes U.S.-Soviet relations of the late 1940's?

A. A climate of escalating tensions and increasingly hostile rhetoric on either side

B. A cooperative atmosphere of mutual trust and cooperation

C. Both sides remained committed to post-war peace but saw different ways of achieving it

D. Immediate hostility on both sides that pushed the nations towards war

10. Which of the following best describes the Tenure of Office Act?

A. It required Senate approval for the removal of government officials.

B. It was declared unconstitutional by the Supreme Court in 1874.

C. It gave term limits to members of Congress.

D. It limited the president to no more than two, four-year terms.

11. Immigration limits passed by Congress in the 1920s were inspired by:

A. Similar laws in Great Britain, Germany, and Ireland

B. Over population of American cities

C. Fears of polluting the white, Anglo-Saxon Protestant population

D. The rising costs associated with care and education of newly arrived immigrants

12. The British Empire was transformed in the first half of the eighteenth century. Which of the following best describes the effects of this transformation?

A. British power was diluted and severely weakened by colonial obligations.

B. The influence of the British monarchy waned; popular pressure forced the passage of a written constitution.

C. The religious balance of Britain shifted; it became a Catholic nation.

D. Britain became a global military and economic power.

13. Italy (from 1922 to 1945), the USSR, Nazi Germany, and present-day North Korea are all examples of:

    A. Ronald Regan's "Evil Empire."

    B. Fascist governments.

    C. Totalitarian countries.

    D. Communist states.

14. In Leninism, socialism is immediately preceded by:

    A. Marxist-Leninism (i.e. Communism).

    B. Bourgeois capitalism.

    C. A democratically organized Dictatorship of the Proletariat.

    D. Rebellion and revolt.

15. Colonial resistance to British rule occasioned harsh penalties by British officials throughout the 1760s and 1770s. Which of the following best describes the opposition to British rule at the start of the Revolutionary War?

    A. The British were universally hated and feared in the American colonies.

    B. Resistance to British authority was strongest among large plantation owners of the south

    C. Northern merchants rejected discriminatory British tax policies but depended too heavily on British trade to upset the balance.

    D. Popular opinion was inconsistent and divided at the start.

Read the following extract from George Fitzhugh's pamphlet "Slavery Justified" (1849) to answer the three questions that follow.

At the slaveholding South all is peace, quiet, plenty and contentment. We have no mobs, no trades unions, no strikes for higher wages, no armed resistance to the law, but little jealousy of the rich by the poor. We have but few in our jails, and fewer in our poor houses. We produce enough of the comforts and necessaries of life for a population three or four times as numerous as ours. We are wholly exempt from the torrent of pauperism, crime, agrarianism, and infidelity which Europe is pouring from her jails and alms houses on the already crowded North.

Population increases slowly, wealth rapidly. In the tide water region of Eastern Virginia, as far as our experience extends, the crops have doubled in fifteen years, whilst the population has been almost stationary. In the same period the lands, owing to improvements of the soil and the many fine houses erected in the country, have nearly doubled in value. This ratio of improvement has been approximated or exceeded wherever in the South slaves are numerous. We have enough for the present, and no Malthusian specters frightening us for the future. Wealth is more equally distributed than at the North, where a few millionaires own most of the property of the country. (These millionaires are men of cold hearts and weak minds; they know how to make money, but not how to use it, either for the benefit of themselves or of others.)

High intellectual and moral attainments, refinement of head and heart, give standing to a man in the South, however poor he may be. Money is, with few exceptions, the only thing that ennobles at the North. We have poor among us, but none who are over-worked and under-fed. We do not crowd cities because lands are abundant and their owners kind, merciful and hospitable. The poor are as hospitable as the rich, the negro as the white man. Nobody dreams of turning a friend, a relative, or a stranger from his door. The very negro who deems it no crime to steal, would scorn to sell his hospitality. We have no loafers, because the poor relative or friend who borrows our horse, or spends a week under our roof, is a welcome guest. The loose economy, the wasteful mode of living at the South, is a blessing when rightly considered; it keeps want, scarcity and famine at a distance, because it leaves room for retrenchment.

16. How does the author defend slavery?

A. Slavery is a self-evident condition inherent of all great powers. Without it, America would surely fall under the influence of some foreign government.

B. The inherent peacefulness of southern life allows a simple but comfortable lifestyle.

C. Southerners recognize class distinction; slavery fits very well within preconceived ideas of social separation.

D. He claims that slavery has diffused the population and allowed southerners to do more with less.

17. Which of the following best represents the author's view of northerners?

A. Northerners have wasteful habits and do not know how to save their money.

B. Northerners seem predisposed to an uneven distribution of wealth.

C. Most northerners are wealthy and corrupt.

D. Northern agriculture is behind the times; this has created poverty and greed.

18. Which of the following points argued by the author is the most easily refuted?

A. His argument that southerners are not crowded into cities.

B. The idea that wealth in the South is evenly distributed.

C. His contention that southerners are hospitable and friendly towards one another

D. His argument that the southern population grew slowly.

19. Historians and economists now see the crises of the savings and loan industry for the 1980s as evidence that:

A. The banking system is prone to violent corrective swings without cause of warning

B. Proof that capitalism works best in a deregulated environment

C. A policy of government deregulation does not work

D. Proof that the average American lacks the financial wherewithal to look out for their own interests

20. How did President Roosevelt respond to the 1902 strike by the United Mine Workers?

A. When the owners refused to come to the bargaining table he threatened to send federal troops in to seize the mines.

B. Roosevelt asked to arbitrate the issue himself. The United Mine Workers accepted but the managers of the mine did not. Roosevelt had to threaten legal action for them to relent.

C. Popular opinion seemed to indicate that no measure taken by the president would be viewed favorably. Roosevelt decided to do nothing and the issue resolved itself within a few months.

D. Roosevelt asked the Chairman of the Federal Reserve to lower interest rates to managers of the mine. Reduced rates of interest would, he argued; greatly improve the situation of striking workers.

Read the following excerpt from Machiavelli's *The Prince* (Cir. 1513) and answer the four questions that follow.

Every one understands how praiseworthy it is in a prince to keep faith, and to live uprightly and not craftily. Nevertheless we see, from what has taken place in our own days, that princes who have set little store by their word, but have known how to overreach men by their cunning, have accomplished great things, and in the end got the better of those who trusted to honest dealing.

Be it known, then, that there are two ways of contending, — one in accordance with the laws, the other by force; the first of which is proper to men, the second to beasts. But since the first method is often ineffectual, it becomes necessary to resort to the second. A prince should, therefore, understand how to use well both the man and the beast. . . . But inasmuch as a prince should know how to use the beast's nature wisely, he ought of beasts to choose both the lion and the fox; for the lion cannot guard himself from the toils, nor the fox from wolves. He must therefore be a fox to discern toils, and a lion to drive off wolves.

To rely wholly on the lion is unwise; and for this reason a prudent prince neither can nor ought to keep his word when to keep it is hurtful to him and the causes which led him to pledge it are removed. If all men were good, this would not be good advice, but since they are dishonest and do not keep faith with you, you in return need not keep faith with them; and no prince was ever at a loss for plausible reasons to cloak a breach of faith. Of this numberless recent instances could be given, and it might be shown how many solemn treaties and engagements have been rendered inoperative and idle through want of faith among princes, and that he who has best known how to play the fox has had the best success.

21. What place does religion have in the rule of a prince?

A. It is of vital importance; only the divinely inspired ruler will maintain the approval of the people.

B. It is important to pay the proper respects to clerics and, most importantly, the Pope.

C. It is necessary to cultivate the appearance of religion, what the Prince does in his private life is immaterial.

D. Very little, princes are more effective when they rely on their own intelligence and cunning.

22. Which of the following best describes Machiavelli's advice on the use of intimidation and physical force?

A. Force is almost always unnecessary, threats of force, however, should be used whenever the need arises.

B. People respond only to violence, there is no need to cultivate any other habits or abilities.

C. A prince must understand when to use the law and when to take matters into his own hands.

D. Violence is useful but not always required.

23. What larger historical theme is this work apart?

A. The failures of absolute monarchs to maintain power in the sixteenth century.

B. The tenuous situation of early-modern Italian city-states.

C. The rise of a literary elite.

D. The declining power of the papacy.

24. Which of the following best describes this work?

A. A work of secular humanism typical of the Renaissance.

B. A political treatise not unlike others of the Enlightenment.

C. Part of the Romantic movement of Continental Europe.

D. An outlier, dissimilar in everyway from its contemporaries.

Read the passages below concerning the debate over the ratification of the Constitution and answer the two questions that follow.

Passage A

The chief advantages which have been urged in favor of Unity in the Executive, are the Secrecy, the Dispatch, the Vigor and Energy which the Government will derive from it; especially in time of War. That these are great Advantages, I shall most really allow. They have been strongly insisted on by all monarchical Writers, they have been acknowledged by the ablest and most candid Defenders of Republican Government; and it cannot be denied that a Monarchy possesses them in a much greater Degree than a Relic. Yet perhaps a little Reflection may incline us to doubt whether these advantages are not greater in Theory than in Practice lead us to enquire whether there is not some prevailing Principle in Republican Government, which sets at Naught, and tramples upon this boasted Superiority . . . . [The] invincible Principle is to be found in the Love the Affection the Attachment of the Citizens to their laws, to their Freedom, and to their Country. Every Husbandman will be quickly converted into a Soldier, when he knows and feels that he is to fight not in defense of the Rights of a particular Family, or a Prince; but for his own . . . . It was this which, in ancient times, enabled the little cluster of Grecian Republics to resist and almost constantly to defeat the Persian Monarch. It was this which supported the States of Holland against a Body of veteran Troops through a Thirty Years War with Spain, then the greatest Monarchy in Europe and finally rendered them victorious.

Passage B

It is not a new observation that the people of any country (if, like the Americans, intelligent and well informed) seldom adopt and steadily persevere for many years in an erroneous opinion respecting their interests. That consideration naturally tends to create great respect for the high opinion which the people of America have so long and uniformly entertained of the importance of their continuing firmly united under one federal government, vested with sufficient powers for all general and national purposes . . . . Among the many objects to which a wise and free people find it necessary to direct their attention, that of providing for their safety seems to be the first. The safety of the people doubtless has relation to a great variety of circumstances and considerations, and consequently affords great latitude to those who wish to define it precisely and comprehensively . . . . The number of wars which have happened or will happen in the world will always be found to be in proportion to the number and weight of the causes, whether real or pretended, which provoke or invite them. If this remark be just, it becomes useful to inquire whether so many just causes of war are likely to be given by united as by disunited America; for if it should turn out that United America will probably give the fewest, then it will follow that in this respect the Union tends most to preserve the people in a state of peace with other nations.

25. What aspect of the Constitution do these authors debate?

    A. The law making power of the legislative branch.

    B. War powers of president.

    C. The right to bear arms.

    D. Duties of the supreme and federal courts.

26. Both authors make use of historical president to defend their arguments. Which of the following best explains their approaches?

    A. Passage A is concerned with a more accurate representation of facts; Passage B addresses only those aspects that prove the argument.

    B. Passage A describes war as a personal and individual choice; Passage B presents a top-down interpretation of causality.

    C. Passage A demonstrates the "great man" theory of history; Passage B is more balanced in its portrayal.

    D. Passage A looks to define the significance of warfare; Passage B treats significance as though it were an assumed fact.

27. Which of the following situations is best explained by economic scarcity theory?

A. A case where demand far exceeds available supply

B. Seasonal variations in prices

C. Fluctuations in the marker for luxury items

D. A price for commodities that rises and falls with demand

28. The spread of Mesopotamian culture in the third millennium BCE is credited mostly to:

A. The invention of pictograph writing

B. Advanced trade networks

C. The conquests of the Akkadians

D. The development of the flatbottom boat

29. Us the following statement to answer the question that follows:

Senator Smith's position on illegal immigration is simply illogical and a product, no doubt, of his own corrupted sense of morality. How can a man, who has fathered a child out of wedlock and declared personal bankruptcy, argue for more restrictive laws?

This statement represents:

A. An ad homonym attack

B. Gentle persuasion

C. A deductive argument

D. An argument by analogy

30. The Panic of 1873 led to more than 10,000 business failures, massive unemployment, and deflation. Where did the Panic originate?

A. Wall Street investment banks

B. Southern textile mills

C. European financers

D. Protectionist trade policies initiated by the federal government

31. Which of the following best describes the religious difference between Native American and European colonists?

A. Native Americans entrusted spiritual authority to priest-like leaders not an entire body of believers.

B. Native Americans celebrated religious festivals and ceremonial religious rights, colonists did not.

C. European colonists attached religious significance to all living beings; natives understood spirituality only in human terms.

D. European colonists valued religious shrines, temples, and other holy places. Native Americans did not understand how spirituality could reside in a geographic location.

32. The principal concern of Taoist philosopher Laozi was:

    A. The moral duty rulers had to their subjects

    B. A balance between the yin and yang, complementary female and male natures

    C. Creating a place for philosophers in the hierarchy of political leadership

    D. Ending wars through the observance of nature

33. Use the list below to answer the question that follows:

Moral Majority
Censorship of media
Outlawing abortion
Small government
Deregulation of commerce

All of the above can be associated with the:

    A. Religious Right of the 1980s

    B. Democratic party of the 1970s

    C. Libertarian party of the 1980s

    D. Republican party of the 1980s

34. Unlike a free market economy, a command economy:

    A. Is controlled by a single government entity or ruler

    B. Is less restrictive due to price controls

    C. Produces only as many goods are demanded by the public

    D. Resources are allocated according to a mixture of government and public decisions

35. The Epic of Gilgamesh is believed to contain the first:

    A. Legal Code of ancient Mesopotamia

    B. Account of a world-wide flood

    C. Description of Sumerian gods and goddesses

    D. Detailed account of the afterlife

Use the following excerpt from Rudyard Kipling's poem *The White Man's Burden: The United States and the Philippine Islands* (1899) to answer the three questions that follow.

Take up the White Man's burden--
Send forth the best ye breed--
Go bind your sons to exile
To serve your captives' need;
To wait in heavy harness,
On fluttered folk and wild--
Your new-caught, sullen peoples,
Half-devil and half-child.

Take up the White Man's burden--
In patience to abide,
To veil the threat of terror
And check the show of pride;
By open speech and simple,
An hundred times made plain
To seek another's profit,
And work another's gain.

Take up the White Man's burden--
The savage wars of peace--
Fill full the mouth of Famine
And bid the sickness cease;
And when your goal is nearest
The end for others sought,
Watch sloth and heathen Folly
Bring all your hopes to nought.

Take up the White Man's burden--
No tawdry rule of kings,
But toil of serf and sweeper--
The tale of common things.
The ports ye shall not enter,
The roads ye shall not tread,
Go mark them with your living,
And mark them with your dead.

Take up the White Man's burden--
Have done with childish days--
The lightly proferred laurel,
The easy, ungrudged praise.
Comes now, to search your manhood
Through all the thankless years
Cold, edged with dear-bought wisdom,
The judgment of your peers!

36. What is the main argument of "White Man's Burden"?

A. Imperialism is justified

B. Wars of aggression are never acceptable

C. America was on the decline

D. European empires are as strong as ever

37. What are the duties of those tasked with the "White Man's Burden"?

A. Rule over and encourage the social and cultural development of countries settled by non-White Europeans

B. Trade freely with other nations, encourage competition, and seek racial harmony through commerce

C. Treat those from other cultures and backgrounds fairly lest you fall victim to racism

D. Christian love is all that is required. Promote Christianity and you will promote peace on earth

38. How does Kipling portray non-Whites?

A. He is even-handed in his portrayal, pointing out the positive and negative qualities of other races.

B. Non-whites are heathens, given to sloth and indolence.

C. They are clever and more industrious than Northern Europeans

D. Kipling says almost nothing about the character, cultural or otherwise, of non-White peoples.

39. Which of the following best describes the reaction of American colonists at the conclusion of the French and Indian War?

A. Colonists hated the British and wanted them out of the colonies.

B. Popular sentiment turned against British loyalists and the majority of Americans wanted war.

C. Colonial leaders pressed for the protection of the Spanish and argued for war with France.

D. There was an immediate surge of British pride in the American colonies.

40. All the following were projects sponsored by Franklin D. Roosevelt's depression-era policies, except:

A. Construction on roads, bridges, and dams

B. Murals, symphonies, plays and other artistic displays

C. Histories, archaeological expedition, and state guide books

D. Corporate-run farming aggregates, agricultural colleges, and money for new agricultural technologies

41. On a map longitude specifies:

A. The north-south orientation of a physical location.

B. The east-west location of a place on the globe.

C. The point nearest to "true north" (+180°) on a compass.

D. The division between eastern and western hemispheres.

42. The agreement whereby farmers agreed to work a piece of land in exchange for ½ of the yearly profits is known as:

A. Contracting

B. Sharecropping

C. Title-holding

D. Shareholding

Read the following excerpt from Pericles' Funeral Oration (cir. 430 BCE) and answer the two questions that follow.

Our form of government does not enter into rivalry with the institutions of others. We do not copy our neighbors, but are an example to them. We are called a democracy, for the administration is in the hands of the many, not of the few. But while the law secures equal justice to all alike in their private disputes, the claim of excellence is also recognized; and when a citizen is in any way distinguished he is preferred to the public service, not as a matter of privilege, but as the reward of merit. . . .

Since we do not anticipate the pain, although, when the hour comes, we can be as brave as those who never allow themselves to rest; and thus, too, our city is equally admirable in peace and in war. For we are lovers of the beautiful, yet simple in our tastes, and we cultivate the mind without loss of manliness. Riches we employ as means to action, not for boasting and display. To avow poverty with us is no disgrace; not to endeavor to escape it by exertion were disgrace indeed. An Athenian citizen does not neglect the state because he takes care of his domestic affairs, and even those who are engaged in agriculture and handicraft labor are possessors of political knowledge. We alone regard a man who takes no interest in public affairs, not as a harmless but as a useless character. . . .

In short, I may affirm that the city at large is the instructress of Greece, and that each sane person among us seems to possess the most ready versatility in adopting himself, and that not ungracefully, to the greatest variety of circumstances and situations that diversify human life.

43. What, according to Pericles, defines the Athenian democracy?

A. Participation by high-minded Athenians.

B. War, violence, and other displays of "manliness."

C. Religious unity and reverence to the gods

D. Wealth and prosperity of Athenian citizens.

44. Which of the following best critiques Pericles' argument?

A. There is no mention of how the recent war with Sparta affected the "circumstances and situations" of everyday life in the city.

B. Athens was militarily strong because if could afford to by allies. Pericles boast of the wealth of the Athenian government but says nothing about how tenuous their hold on power really was.

C. This is an idealized look at Athenian society. Pericles seems ignorant of the greed, selfishness, and political factionalism that undermined Athenian power.

D. Religion was perhaps the main motivating cause of the Athenian people; politics did not influence the daily decisions of its citizens.

45. Use the list below to answer the question that follows:

A "league of nations" that would mutually ensure political stability.
Agreements to end secrete treaties between nations.
Colonial claims by competing parties would be settled by impartial arbitrators.
A drastic reduction in all national armaments.
Open and free trade between nations.

All of the ideas listed above were post-war proposals of this American president:

A. Harry Truman.

B. Woodrow Wilson.

C. Calvin Coolidge.

D. Theodore Roosevelt.

46. In the election of 1912, presidential nominee Theodore Roosevelt supported all of the following, except:

A. Women's suffrage.

B. Regulation of child labor and a minimum wage.

C. Regulation of corporations through a Federal Trade Commission.

D. 2-year term limits for U.S. Congressmen.

47. Which of the following best represents the condition of the earliest settlers in Virginia's Jamestown colony?

A. Life was extraordinarily difficulty but bearable, most lasted through the first winter and went on to achieve great wealth.

B. Early settlers in Jamestown were predominantly male and often elected to abandon the settlement in favor or other, most hospitable surroundings.

C. The discovery of tobacco brought immediate success to the venture; thousands of English settlers found an immediate and lasting source of income.

D. Starvation and Indian attacks threatened to upend the designs of would-be colonialists from the start.

48. America's westward expansion best is best understood by the following geographic theme:

A. Movement

B. Human-environment interaction

C. Location

D. Place

Read the following excerpt from Livy's *History of Rome* and answer the question that follows.

A very large body of Sabines, spreading devastations around, advanced almost to the walls of Rome. The fields were deserted, and the city struck with terror. [The Roman senate] resolved that a dictator should be chosen to extricate them from this distress, and Lucius Quintius Cincinnatus was accordingly appointed with unanimous approbation. Lucius Quintius, the now sole hope of the people, and of the empire of Rome, cultivated a farm of four acres on the other side of the Tiber. There he was found by the deputies, either leaning on a stake, in a ditch which he was making, or plouging; in some work of husbandry he was certainly employed. After wiping the sweat and dust from his brow, he came forward, when the deputies congratulated him, and saluted him dictator; requested his presence in the city, and informed him of the alarming situation of the army. Quintius at first refused the office, and asked them, what they meant by exposing him in the extremity of age to such a violent contest. On which they all joined in asserting, that his aged breast was fraught not only with more wisdom, but with more fortitude also, than was to be found in all the rest. [After defeating the Sabines] Cincinnatus resigned on the sixteenth day the dictatorship which had been conferred upon him for six months.

49. What significance did the story of Cincinnatus hold for Americans in the aftermath of the Revolution?

    A. Cincinnatus showed that even the old could serve with military distinction.

    B. It was used by Federalists to show the necessity of a strong executive branch.

    C. Republicans referred to Cincinnatus as the example of a gentleman farmer.

    D. It represented a pure devotion to one's country, unburdened by politics or self-interest.

50. Why was the medieval Catholic Church so opposed to the practice of lay investiture?

A. Ceremonies where the king 'invested' clergy were held in the palace and therefore unholy.

B. Lay investiture made it seem as though secular rulers, not the papacy, were the source of spiritual power.

C. Lay investiture made clergy liable to taxation by secular rulers.

D. The practice bound clergy to the secular authority of kings and noblemen.

51. Which of the following may be said of the interaction between Neanderthals and Cro-Magnons?

A. Cro-Magnons preceded Neanderthals by about 100,000 years

B. Both species interacted for around 50,000 years until Neanderthals died out

C. The earliest Cro-Magnons are found primarily in Africa. The origins of Neanderthals is slightly more obscure

D. Neanderthals evolved into Cro-Magnons around 200,000 years ago

52. The Truman Doctrine intended to convince Americans of the need to:

A. Abandon hopes for nuclear disarmament in the new post-war world

B. Support "free peoples" of the world through direct financial assistance

C. Devote more money to defense spending

D. Contribute directly to the reconstruction of war-torn Europe

53. Early Celtic tribes remained separate and distinct except in their respect for:

A. The half-dozen gods and goddesses that made up the Celtic pantheon

B. Roman culture

C. Roman authority

D. The authority of Druid priests

54. What is the distinguishing feature of homo habilis?

A. Cultivation of crops

B. Settled habitation

C. The discovery of fire

D. The use and production of tools

Read the following excerpt, adapted from the *Bhagavad Gita* (cir. 5th to 2nd century BCE) to answer the two questions that follow.

The Deity said [to Arjuna]: You have grieved for those who deserve no grief, and you speak words of wisdom. Learned men grieve not for the living nor the dead. Never did I not exist, nor you, nor these rulers of men; nor will any one of us ever hereafter cease to be. As in this body, infancy and youth and old age (come) to the embodied (self), so does the acquisition of another body; a sensible man is not deceived about that. The contacts of the senses which produce cold and heat, pleasure and pain, are not permanent, they are for ever coming and going. Bear them for that sensible man whom they afflict not, (pain and pleasure being alike to him), he merits immortality. There is no existence for that which is unreal; there is no non-existence for that which is real. And the (correct) conclusion about both is perceived by those who perceive the truth.

Know that to be indestructible which pervades all this; the destruction of that inexhaustible (principle) none can bring about these bodies appertaining to the embodied (self) which is eternal, indestructible, and indefinable, are declared to be perishable; therefore do engage in battle. He who thinks one to be the killer and he who thinks one to be the killed both know nothing. He kills not, is not killed. He is not born, nor does he ever die, nor, having existed, does he exist no more. Unborn, everlasting, unchangeable, and very ancient, he is not killed when the body is killed. . . . As a man, casting off old clothes, puts on others and new ones, so the embodied (self), casting off old bodies, goes to others and new ones.

This embodied (self), O descendant of Bharata! within every one's body is ever indestructible. Therefore you ought not to grieve for any being. Having regard to your own duty also, you ought not to falter, for there is nothing better for a member of your station than a righteous battle. But if you will not fight this righteous battle, then you will have abandoned your own duty and your fame, and you will incur sin. All beings, too, will tell of your everlasting infamy; and to one who has been honored, infamy is (a) greater (evil) than death. Warriors will think that you abstained from the battle through fear, and having been highly thought of by them, you will fall down to littleness.

55. What does this passage help explain?

A. Humans were put on earth to kill one another.

B. Life is full of random and unexplainable events.

C. The purpose of life is to fulfill your duty, an unavoidable and permanent constant in the universe.

D. A heroic death is all that one can hope for. Battle brings permanent glory, cowardice, and eternal shame.

56. What do we learn about the nature of existence?

A. Our physical form is immaterial to the business of living.

B. Only warriors must worry about the physical life and death of their bodies.

C. Our bodies are the only permanent part of our being.

D. Our self-image is the only true constant.

57. President John Adams and members of the Federalist party argued that a strong central government was necessary because:

A. All humans were driven by self-interest. This had the tendency to create conflict in the absence of a powerful mediator

B. Americans needed an aristocracy based on the British model

C. American businesses were slowly beginning to dominate state governments

D. Power vested in the hands of a hereditary monarch was always more acceptable to the masses

58. Hadrian's Wall, a defensive structure built by Roman soldiers in the 2nd Century CE, stretches 73 miles across:

A. Northern England

B. Northern Ireland

C. The French-Spanish boarder

D. The Southern coast of Italy

59. The invasion of Grenada by United States marines in 1983 was part of a larger effort to:

A. Protect Grenada's ailing sugar and tobacco industries

B. Overthrow a cruel and unpopular dictatorship

C. Stop the rise of Communism in Central America

D. Control the balance of trade in the Western Hemisphere

60. Which of the following best explains the militarism of the Spartan city-state circa 460 BCE?

A. Defensive struggles against Phoenicians and Greek city-states left them no choice but to mobilize all adult males for military service

B. Spartan slaves, otherwise known as Helots, overwhelmed the free populace. The threat of a slave uprising required a strong domestic military presence.

C. The duel-kingship system of shared authority led to internecine civil wars and created a climate of distrust

D. Early defeats at the hands of the Persians took Sparta from a peaceful to a warlike state of political existence

61. This subspecies of homo erectus were the primary occupants of Europe to 40,000 BCE:

A. Homo sapiens

B. Homo habilis

C. Homo erectus

D. Neanderthals

62. The first ten amendments to the U.S. Constitution are better known as the:

A. Preamble

B. Separation of Powers

C. Bill of Rights

D. Articles

63. The New Deal dramatically altered the way:

A. Americans felt about government assistance

B. African-Americans fought for civil rights

C. American businesses interacted with one another

D. American politicians campaigned for office

64. Prairies, pampas, steppes, and savannas are all:

A. Grasslands.

B. Areas that receive less that 10 inches of rain a year.

C. Watersheds

D. Littoral regions

65. What were the two most important aspects of the "Columbian Exchange"?

A. Religion and gold

B. Epidemics and food

C. Tobacco and coffee

D. Technology and spices

66. Cardinal Richelieu is considered by historians to have been the power behind Louis XIII. He is mainly remembered for:

A. His promotion of French nobility.

B. His efforts to strengthen the French monarchy.

C. The religious freedoms he extended to French Huguenots.

D. The corruption and greed that he introduced to the French court.

Read the following excerpt from the French Edict of 1626 and answer the question that follows.

Whereas formerly the assemblies of the estates of this realm and those of notable persons chosen to give advice to ourselves, and to the late king, our very honorable lord and father, on important affairs of this realm, and likewise the assembly of the estates of the province of Brittany held by us in the year 1614, have repeatedly requested and very humbly supplicated our said lord and father and ourselves to cause the demolition of many strongholds in divers places of this realm, which, being neither on hostile frontiers nor in important passes or places, only serve to augment our expenses by the maintenance of useless garrisons, and also serve as retreats for divers persons who on the least provocation disturb the provinces where they are located; . . .

For these reasons, we announce, declare, ordain, and will that all the strongholds, either towns or castles, which are in the interior of our realm or provinces of the same, not situated in places of importance either for frontier defense or other considerations of weight, shall be razed and demolished; even ancient walls shall be destroyed so far as it shall be deemed necessary for the well-being and repose of our subjects and the security of this state, so that our said subjects henceforth need not fear that the said places will cause them any inconvenience, and so that we shall be freed from the expense of supporting garrisons in them.

67. How might have the Edict influenced French society in the 17th century?

A. It strengthened the position of the French monarchy.

B. It weakened the frontier defenses of France

C. It opened a new era of cross-border trade and cultural exchange

D. The position of the French nobility was greatly improved.

68. This mountain range runs from southern New Mexico to the Northernmost part of British Columbia:

A. Pacific Coast Range

B. Cascade Range

C. Sierra Nevada

D. Rocky Mountains

69. How was power divided in the Roman Republic?

A. Among a series of King and regional military leaders

B. Between the Roman Senate, counsels, and various other assemblies

C. Between the senate representing the interests of the wealthy, and plebian's, a council representing Roman poor

D. The Pontifix Maximus, chief priest, was the head of state

70. A country's standard of living is usually assessed by this economic measurement:

A. The rate of deflation

B. The duration of business cycle

C. Jobless rate

D. Gross Domestic Product

71. Democracy failed to take hold in many post-colonial African states because:

A. Democracy was a foreign, and mostly unknown, political institution

B. Strong African Kings, dictators, and warlords saw democracy as a challenge to their authority

C. Independent African businesses could not keep pace with the modern economy

D. Colonial rulers left a legacy of paternalism and authoritarian

Use the following excerpt from Karl Marx's *18th Brumaire of Louise Bonaparte* (1852) to answer the three questions that follow.

Man makes his own history, but he does not make it out of the whole cloth; he does not make it out of conditions chosen by himself, but out of such as he finds close at hand. The tradition of all past generations weighs like a nightmare upon the brain of the living. At the very time when men appear engaged in revolutionizing things and themselves, in bringing about what never was before, at such very epochs of revolutionary crises do they anxiously conjure up into their service the spirits of the past, assume their names, their battle cries, their costumes to enact a new historic scene in such time-honored disguise and with such borrowed language. Thus did Luther masquerade as the Apostle Paul; thus did the revolution of 1789-1814 drape itself alternately as Roman Republic and as Roman Empire; nor did the revolution of 1848 know what better to do than to parody at one time the year 1789, at another the revolutionary traditions of 1793-95. Thus does the beginner, who has acquired a new language, keep on translating it back into his own mother tongue; only then has he grasped the spirit of the new language and is able freely to express himself therewith when he moves in it without recollections of old, and has forgotten in its use his own hereditary tongue.

When these historic conjurations of the dead past are closely observed a striking difference is forthwith noticeable. Camille Desmoulins, Danton, Robespierre, St. Juste, Napoleon, the heroes as well as the parties and the masses of the old French revolution, achieved in Roman costumes and with Roman phrases the task of their time: the emancipation and the establishment of modern bourgeois society. One set knocked to pieces the old feudal groundwork and mowed down the feudal heads that had grown upon it; Napoleon brought about, within France, the conditions under which alone free competition could develop, the partitioned lands be exploited, the nation's unshackled powers of industrial production be utilized; while, beyond the French frontier, he swept away everywhere the establishments of feudality, so far as requisite, to furnish the bourgeois social system of France with fit surroundings of the European continent, and such bourgeois revolutions, like those of the eighteenth century, rush onward rapidly from success to success, their stage effects outbid one another, men and things seem to be set in flaming brilliants, ecstasy is the prevailing spirit; but they are short-lived, they reach their climax speedily, then society relapses into a long fit of nervous reaction before it learns how to appropriate the fruits of its period of feverish excitement.

Proletarian revolutions, on the contrary, such as those of the nineteenth century, criticize themselves constantly; constantly interrupt themselves in their own course; come back to what seems to have been accomplished, in order to start over anew; scorn with cruel thoroughness the half measures, weaknesses and meannesses of their first attempts; seem to throw down their adversary only in order to enable him to draw fresh strength from the earth, and again to rise up against them in more gigantic stature; constantly recoil in fear before the undefined monster magnitude of their own objects. Every observer of average intelligence, even if he failed to follow step by step the course of French development, must have anticipated that an unheard of fiasco was in store for the revolution.

72. What is Marx attempting in the above?

A. A critique of recent reforms in the Catholic Church.

B. To explain the revolutionary history of France.

C. This is an attack on the imperial practices of Napoleon.

D. He is arguing that history is an inappropriate guide to the future.

73. What, according to Marx, are the characteristics of proletariat revolutions?

A. They listen very carefully to the past, hear the wisdom of the ages, and act appropriately.

B. The proletariat are only of "average intelligence" therefore their revolutions are doomed to failure.

C. They occur in fits and starts; revolutionaries are in an almost perpetual state of revolution.

D. They require a strong leader and support of the workers.

74. Why, according to Marx, did the French Revolution fail?

A. It did not fail; this is simply the expected course all revolutions take. Napoleon started the revolution and passed it on to others.

B. It was a bourgeois revolution; revolutionary leaders like Napoleon just replaced one set of bourgeois values (feudalism) with another (industrialism).

C. The French are wholly incapable of sustaining a revolution, their cultural ideals draw too heavily on Roman models.

D. It came on too suddenly and society did not know how to react to it.

75. How did Federalists maintain political influence after the election of 1800?

A. American military commanders were loyal to the Federalist cause. Only those with Federalist loyalties were considered for military rank.

B. Before he left office, President John Adams appointed a number of Federalist judges.

C. Federalist newspaper editors helped to press forward Federalist policies in the west and south.

D. Federalists were a majority in the both houses of Congress.

76. In contrast to landscape ecology, reconciliation ecology places more of a emphasis on:

A. Environmental factors that contribute to biodiversity.

B. Achieving ecological balance in areas of human activity.

C. How spatial structures affect the types of organisms that inhabit a certain area.

D. Interdisciplinary connections between the natural and social sciences.

77. Which of the following best describes the nine U.S. presidents that served between 1837 and 1861 (from Andrew Jackson to Abraham Lincoln)?

A. A series of one-term (or less) presidents that refused to take definitive positions on the issue of slavery.

B. Strong and decisive leaders who dominated all aspects of the federal government.

C. A series of Northern aristocrats who pressed for war with the South at every turn.

D. Each of these men were chosen because of their military service.

78. In his attempt to restore consumer confidence, President Franklin D. Roosevelt promoted a series of:

A. Public forums.

B. “Fireside chats.”

C. Publications aimed at rural farmers.

D. Short movie clips to be played before features.

Read the following excerpt from Thomas Paine's *Common Sense* (1776) and answer the question that follows:

To the evil of monarchy we have added that of hereditary succession; and as the first is a degradation and lessening of ourselves, so the second, claimed as a matter of right, is an insult and imposition on posterity. For all men being originally equals, no one by birth could have a right to set up his own family in perpetual preference to all others for ever, and tho' himself might deserve some decent degree of honors of his contemporaries, yet his descendants might be far too unworthy to inherit them . . . . Secondly, as no man at first could possess any other public honors than were bestowed upon him, so the givers of those honors could have no power to give away the right of posterity, and though they might say "We choose you for our head," they could not without manifest injustice to their children say "that your children and your children's children shall reign over ours forever." Because such an unwise, unjust, unnatural compact might (perhaps) in the next succession put them under the government of a rogue or a fool. Most wise men in their private sentiments have ever treated hereditary right with contempt; yet it is one of those evils which when once established is not easily removed: many submit from fear, others from superstition, and the more powerful part shares with the king the plunder of the rest.

79. What, according to Paine, is the danger of monarchical rule?

A. Successors might be inadequately prepared for leadership.

B. It removes motivation and the creative impulse from society.

C. Hereditary rulers tend to side with members of the aristocracy.

D. Wars are primarily fought between competing monarchs, not free people.

80. President Warren G. Harding and Calvin Coolidge agreed that the role of government was to:

A. Defend the interests of workers

B. Promote private enterprise by ending cronyism and corruption in government

C. Regulate commerce through a vast bureaucratic hierarchy

D. Ensure the productivity and growth of American business

81. How are social histories different from cultural histories?

A. Social histories focus on structures (groups of people in society); cultural histories examine the values, beliefs, and practices of individuals within groups.

B. Social histories are inherently “presentist”; cultural history is static.

C. Cultural histories focus on the larger patterns in history; social histories are concerned only with micro-level historical questions.

D. Cultural histories examine recent history; social histories concern subjects that are at least 30 years in the past.

82. As part of his economic recovery plan, President Ronald Regan:

A. Cut federal assistance programs for the nations poorest citizens

B. Halted the flow of illegal immigrants

C. Increased government spending in health care

D. Pushed for tax breaks to members of the middle class only

83. The Persian bi-metallic (gold and silver) system of coinage had an immediate and dramatic effect on:

A. Commerce; retail markets and the cost of human labor took on new meanings

B. The price of goods; inflation nearly bankrupted the empire

C. Warfare; small but coin rich city states could now hire mercenary armies

D. The power of rulers; by stamping their portraits on coins. Kings and emperors became all powerful

84. Use the list below to answer the question that follows:

An attempt to make the country more self-sufficient.
Support of a national bank and stable currency.
Policies directed toward improving American infrastructure.
A plan to increase foreign tariffs.
Federal control of the price of public land.

The items listed above best describe which of the following?

A. Henry Clay's American System.

B. The first items to be argued before the Supreme Court.

C. Ideas promoted by Southern Republicans during Reconstruction.

D. Bills vetoed by President Andrew Jackson.

85. This English law of 1673 required all those in public office to take an oath to uphold Protestantism (its intent was to keep Catholics out of public office).

A. Act of Rights

B. Defense Act

C. Non-Catholic Act

D. Test Act

86. In order to finance and maintain a strong central government, Federalist such as Alexander Hamilton called for the implementation of this protectionist economic doctrine:

A. Lower restrictions on interstate trade

B. Trade tariffs of foreign imports

C. Taxes on American goods intended for export

D. Increased monetary supply

87. What were the main motivations behind the British assault on Baltimore during the War of 1812?

A. It was America's first capital city and therefore would have forced Americans to give in to all British demands.

B. It was a known base of piracy, the home of American privateers. By capturing the city, the British hoped to end the threat of American piracy.

C. A large community of known British traitors lived there; the British wanted to bring them to trial.

D. Most American munitions stores were located in or near the city of Baltimore.

88. The shaded area below is known as:

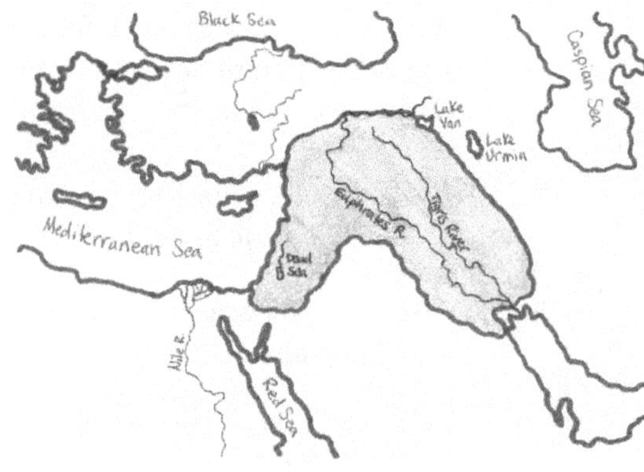

A. The Fertile Crescent

B. Persia

C. The Indus River Valley

D. The Nile River Valley

89. Who put up the money for the first colonial expeditions to the New World?

A. Joint-stock corporations

B. The Catholic Church

C. The Protestant Church

D. The British government

90. Which of the following best characterizes the antebellum Southern economy?

A. It was based primarily on cash crops.

B. It was urban centered with a number of large, densely populated cities.

C. The South was a major producer of textiles.

D. The South was the center of emerging industrial technologies.

91. A map showing areas where earthquakes may cause building damage is most easily developed with the use of:

A. Atlases

B. Aerial surveys

C. Global positioning systems

D. Geographic information systems

92. The nullification crises brought the United States to the brink of civil war in the early 1830s. How was this conflict averted?

A. Congress refused to give President Andrew Jackson the right to use troops to settle the matter.

B. The federal government gave in to Virginia's opposition.

C. South Carolina's army was too much of a challenge for federal troops and the entire issue was dropped.

D. Henry Clay worked a compromise between South Carolina and the federal government.

93. European monarchs in the 15th and 16th centuries ruled under systems of:

A. Royal Absolutism

B. Constitutional Monarchy

C. Dynastic Authority

D. Parliamentary Representation

94. Which of the following was a concession given by Republican leaders in the Compromise of 1877?

A. The promise to remove federal troops from the South.

B. $5 billion in direct federal aid to state governments.

C. A promise to place a Southerner in the presidential cabinet of Rutherford B. Hayes.

D. The right to name ex-confederate general Robert E. Lee Governor of Virginia.

95. How does material culture benefit the study of history?

A. It tells untold stories of the past

B. It allows us insight into the experiences of elites but excludes non-elites

C. Material culture does not benefit the study of history. There is little value in cultural ephemera or cultural artifacts.

D. It provides literal statements of truth that allow unbiased, objective realities

96. Which of the following best explains the rational behind the Marshall Plan?

A. American military bases are the most effective way to diffuse communist military power

B. Basic humanitarian assistance to Europe was a moral issue, not a political one

C. In order to protect against communist influence, America must help rebuild Europe

D. Greece and Turkey were desperate for resources and without American resources, conflict between the nations would be inevitable

97. Unlike the Mesopotamian and the Yangzi Rivers, the Nile River:

A. Was less of a barrier separating early civilizations.

B. Was longer and facilitated greater amounts of cross-cultural exchange in the fourth thru first millennia BCE

C. Allowed for more constant population growth in the fourth thru third millennia BCE

D. Helped propel a ship building book in the second millennia BCE

98. A manufacturing plant where workers are tasked with individual aspects of assembly benefits from the economic theory of:

A. Specialization

B. Piece work

C. Assembly line

D. Just in time production

99. What effect did the geographic location and situation has on the Carthaginian Empire?

A. Volcanic ash gave them nutrient rich soil and allowed for exponential population growth

B. They became advanced seafaring traders but were forced to rely on mercenaries for their armies

C. The lacked raw material and were frequently at war with others to supply those wants

D. Mountainous terrain made them more apt to live in quiet isolation from the rest of the Mediterranean

100. A toy manufacturer decides to produce Frisbees, and earn profit of $10,000. However, the same machinery could be used to produce hula-hoops and earn profit of $15,000. The $5,000 difference is best described as:

A. Debt-to-income ratio

B. Failed resource allocation

C. Price dumping

D. Opportunity cost

Exam 3

Read the passages below related to the Battle of Lexington and Concord and answer the question that follows.

Passage A

Six companies of Light Infantry were detached by Lt Col. Smith to take possession of two bridges on the other side of Concord, near three in the Morning, when we were advanced within about two miles of Lexington, intelligence was received that about 500 men in arms were assembled, determined to oppose the Kings troops, and retard them in their march . . . . On this I gave directions to the troops to move forward, but on no account to fire, or even attempt it without orders; when I arrived at the end of the Village, I observed drawn up upon a Green near 200 rebels; when I came within about 100 yards of them, they began to file off towards some stone walls on our right flank. The Light Infantry, observing this, ran after them. I instantly called to the soldiers not to fire, but surround and disarm them, and after several repetitions of those positive orders to the men, not to fire, etc. some of the rebels who had jumped over the wall fired four or five shots at the soldiers, which wounded a man of the Tenth and my horse was wounded in two places, from some quarter or other, and at the same time several shots were fired from a meeting house on our left. Upon this, without any order or regularity, the Light Infantry began a scattered fire, and continued in that situation for some little time, contrary to the repeated orders both of me and the officers that were present.

Passage B

By the clearest depositions relative to this transaction, it will appear that on the night preceding the 19 of April instant, a body of the king's troops, under the command of Colonel Smith, were secretly landed at Cambridge with an apparent design to take or destroy the military and other stores provided for the defence of this colony, and deposited at Concord that some inhabitants of the colony on the aforesaid, whilst travelling peaceably on the road between Boston were seized and greatly abused by armed men who appeared to be Gage's army; that the town of Lexington by these means was alarmed, and a company of the inhabitants mustered on the occasion; that the regular troops on their way to Concord marched into the said town of Lexington and the said company, on their approach, began to disperse that notwithstanding this, the regulars rushed on with great violence and first began hostilities by firing on said Lexington Company, whereby they killed eight and wounded several others; that the regulars continued their fire until those of said company who were neither killed nor wounded had made their escape; that Colonel Smith with the detachment then marched to Concord, where a number of provincials were again fired on by the troops and two them killed and several wounded, before the provincials fired on them and that these hostile measures of the troops produced an engagement that lasted through the day in which many of the provincials, and more of the regular troops, were killed and wounded.

1. The authors of both passages disagree on:

   A. The location of the battle.

   B. The support of locals.

   C. Which side provoked the battle.

   D. How many British troops fought in the engagement.

2. The Hindenburg, Maginot, and Siegfried lines are all examples of:

   A. Imaginary points on the international date line

   B. Political boundaries separating countries of Eastern Europe

   C. Mountain ranges in Western Europe

   D. Military fortifications built in the 20th Century

3. Which of the following led to Rodger Williams's banishment from the Massachusetts colony?

   A. He rejected the Puritan emphasis on Biblical authority.

   B. He argued for the complete cessation of trade with other colonies.

   C. He purchased vast tracts of land in neighboring Rhode Island without the permission from the Massachusetts General Court.

   D. He argued against the fusion of religion and governmental authority.

4. Which of the following generalization most directly applies to Paleolithic human culture?

   A. Linguistic similarities gave certain groups a decided advantage over others in the hunt for resources

   B. The capacity for symbolic thought is best exemplified by the standardization of tools and cave paintings signify an evolution in human understanding

   C. Organizational habits, such as the development of cities, the means to weigh grain, and hierarchies allowed religion for the so-called Neolithic revolution

   D. New tools and technologies are evidence of trade networks and cross-cultural interaction

5. The nation-wide consumer boycott was first used by:

   A. Unionized Farm workers

   B. Members of the auto industry

   C. Chicago meat-packing unions

   D. Craft and Trade unions of the early 20th Century

6. The village of Catal Huyuk remains the best-preserved example of:

   A. Neolithic settlements

   B. Religious practices of the Paleolithic era

   C. Commercial trade in the Greek Dark Ages

   D. Hellenistic culture

7. Use the list below to answer the question that follows.

A defined racial hierarchy The United States' obligation to instruct members of the developing world Fears of mixing Anglo-Saxon's with other races Competition and expansion

All of the preceding are elements of which Gilded Age philosophy?

   A. Social Darwinism

   B. Fascism

   C. Eugenics

   D. Marxism

8. At its height, the Roman Empire had possessions that completely surrounded this inland sea:

   A. The Black Sea

   B. The Caspian Sea

   C. The Mediterranean Sea

   D. The North Sea

9. Glaciology, the study of ice glaciers, is best approached through the use of:

   A. Atlases and maps.

   B. Satellite imagery and information pulled from geographic databases.

   C. A compass.

   D. Remote sensing equipment.

Use the passage below to answer the three questions that follow.

In order to guard against a too great pinch of starvation he gave them permission to steal this thing or that in the effort to alleviate their hunger. It was not of curse from any real need to supply them with nutrients that he left it to them to provide themselves by this crafty method. Nor can I conceive that any one will so misinterpret the custom. Clearly its explanation lies in the fact that he who would live the life of a robber must forgo sleep by night and in the daytime he must lie in wait for an eventual theft; he must prepare and make ready his scouts, and so forth, if he is to succeed in capturing the prize.

It is obvious, I say, that the whole of this education tended, and was intended, to make the boys craftier and more inventive in getting in supplies, whilst at the same time it cultivated their warlike instincts. An objector may retort: "But if he thought it so fine a feat to steal, why did he inflict all those blows on the unfortunate who was caught?" My answer is: for the self-same reason which induces people, in other matters which are taught, to punish ill-performance. So they, the Lacedaemonians, visit penalties on the boy who is detected thieving as being but a sorry bungler in the art. So to steal as many cheeses as possible was a feat to be encouraged; but, at the same moment, others were enjoined to scourge the thief, which would point a moral not obscurely, that by pain endured for a brief season a man may earn the joyous reward of lasting glory. Herein, too, it is plainly shown that where speed is required, the sluggard will win for himself much trouble and little good.

Furthermore he gave to any citizen who happened to be present, authority to give them instructions for their good, and to scold them for any errors they committed. By so doing he created in the boys a rare modesty and reverence. And indeed there is nothing which, whether as boys or men, they respect more highly than the ruler. Lastly, and with the same intention, that the boys must never be without a ruler.

10. What is the main purpose of this passage?

A. To explain the lawlessness of this society; thefts, robberies, and other malfeasance is part of their culture.

B. The intention is simply to describe the harsh lives of young males so as to gain support for reform.

C. The author is boasting of the hardships endured to make a larger point about the character of a people.

D. The author is convinced that these people are without morality. In the absence of law, they steal. Only when an external authority is present do they behave.

11. Which of the following best describes the virtues of this society?

A. They are devious and without defined moral boundaries yet they depend on each other for the basic necessities of life.

B. This society is closely knit together by shared traditions and customs.

C. They are rugged individualists who maintain complex codes of honor and morality.

D. They prize learning and mentorship above all else.

12. What steps could a historian take to ensure the authenticity of this source?

    A. Find the date of this document and look to see how other accounts from this period and location (concerning youths, family, or punishments) measure up.

    B. Research the author and examine the legitimacy of other, unrelated works.

    C. Check the internal consistency of this source; is the depiction of life, learning, and punishment described in a similar way throughout?

    D. If the work is a translation, parse key words and phrases to identify obvious errors before proceeding.

13. The Alien and Sedition Acts attempted to:

A. Silence political opposition.

B. Extend the rule of law to government officials from foreign countries.

C. End the two-party system.

D. Balance the interests of the state and federal governments.

14. Early tensions between Native Americans and European colonists erupted over which of the following concerns?

A. Native Americans had difficulty adapting to European colonists ideas of private property.

B. Access to the fur trade inspired competition between European merchants and Native American tribal chiefs.

C. Over time, Native American hunting grounds encroached on the pre-established boundaries of colonial settlements.

D. European colonists refused to acknowledge the dominion of a Native American confederation organized in the late 1600s.

15. Which of the following best describes the role of American women during World War II?

A. Women took positions of corporate leadership or jobs that did not require much, if any, physical labor

B. Women were strongly encouraged to participate in factories at the start, but when the war came to an end they were forced to return to traditional occupation

C. Women were mostly restricted to jobs in the service industry or other traditionally female occupations, such as teaching and nursing

D. Women participated in all sectors of the economy and these roles expanded greatly in the years immediately following the end of the war

16. Technological advances in the 1980s and 90s benefited most directly from:

A. Reagan-era tax cuts

B. A burgeoning software industry

C. The move from mainframe computing to personal computing

D. The development of coaxial cable

Read the following extract from Eusebius's *Eccleastical History* (written circa 330 CE) and answer the four questions that follow.

Constantine, the pious son of a most pious and virtuous father, and Licinius next to him, were both in great esteem for their moderation and piety. These two pious rulers had been excited by God, the universal sovereign, against the two most profane tyrants, and engaging in battle, in an extraordinary manner, Maxentius fell under Constantine. But the other, (Maximinus) did not long survive him, being himself put to a most ignominious death, by Licinius, who had not yet at that time evinced his insanity. But Constantine, who was first both in dignity and imperial rank, first took compassion upon those who were oppressed at Rome, invoking the God of heaven, and his Son and word our Lord Jesus Christ, the Saviour of all, as his aid advanced with his whole army, purporting to restore the Romans to that liberty which they had derived from their ancestors.

Maxentius, however, did not venture to advance beyond the gates of the city, but fortified every place and region and city, with vast numbers of soldiers and innumerable bands and garrisons in all places of Rome and Italy that were enslaved by him. But the emperor (Constantine) stimulated by the divine assistance, proceeded against the tyrant, and defeating him without difficulty in the first, second, and third engagements, he advanced through the greatest part of Italy, and came almost to the very gates of Rome. Then, however, that he might not be forced to wage war with the Romans for the sake of the tyrant, God himself drew the tyrant, as if bound in fetters, to a considerable distance from the gates; and here he confirmed those miraculous events performed of old against the wicked, and which have been discredited by so many, as if belonging to fiction and fable, but which have been established in the sacred volume, as credible to the believer.

He confirmed them, I say, as true, by an immediate interposition of his power, addressed alike I may say to the eyes of believers and unbelievers. As, therefore, anciently in the days of Moses, and the religious people of the Hebrews, the chariots of Pharaoh, and his forces were cast into the Red Sea, and his chosen triple combatants were overwhelmed in it; thus, also, Maxentius, and his combatants and guards about him, sunk into the depths like a stone, when he fled before the power of God that was with Constantine, and passed through the river in his way, over which he had formed a bridge by joining boats, and thus prepared the means of his own destruction.

17. To what, according to the author, did Constantine owe his victory over Maxentius?

    A. Superior military forces.

    B. The good will of the people of Rome.

    C. The favor of the Christian God.

    D. The public's hatred of they tyrant Maxentius.

18. How might we interpret Eusebius' motivations for writing this?

    A. He was an imperial propagandist attempting to bolster Constantine's claims for legitimacy.

    B. To curry favor with the a new Roman Emperor

    C. He was arguing that Christianity was the basis for imperial authority.

    D. He wished only to end tyrannical uses of power.

19. What event did this document help to inspire.

    A. The third century invasions.

    B. The imperial law banning all non-Christian religious activity.

    C. The permanent reign of Christian Roman emperors.

    D. The fusion of the Christian Church with imperial interests.

20. Why does Eusebius invoke the image of Constantine as a liberator "purporting to restore the Romans to that liberty which they had derived from their ancestors"?

    A. He is defending the idea that Rome has, and always been a republic.

    B. The hero vs. tyrant metaphor is found throughout classical literature. It is a common convention.

    C. He is attempting to prove that Christian monotheism is the original and truest form of Roman religion.

    D. Eusebius hopes to draw parallels between Constantine and Jesus Christ

21. The Klondike gold rush occurred in the:

A. 17th Century

B. 20th Century

C. 18th Century

D. 19th Century

22. This ex-gladiator led a force of over 70,000 slaves and peasants in a series of raids of the Italian countryside between 73 and 71 BC.

A. Spartacus

B. Gaius Marius

C. Julius Caesar

D. Attila the Hun

23. How did the Cold War alter U.S. military policy?

A. Espionage and secrecy became invaluable assets

B. U.S. Forces ceased cooperation with foreign military allies

C. The developing world became the central focus of military concern

D. Limited conflict replaced total war and diplomacy, not military victories became the norm

24. Which of the following most directly contributed to the end of apartheid in South Africa

A. Condemnations of the white government by members of the western media

B. Boycotts by foreign banks and commercial entities

C. Massive riots and threats of violence against the South African government

D. The move away from a democratically controlled legislative body

25. In American early steamboat traffic had the most dramatic affect on trade along the:

A. Panama Canal

B. Atlantic Coast

C. Mississippi River

D. Gulf of Mexico

26. Use the list below to answer the question that follows:

The Nye Committee
Concerns over a sluggish economy
Dissatisfaction with results of WWI

All of the above were associated with:

A. The American isolationist movement of the 1930's

B. The American labor movement of the 1920's

C. American foreign diplomacy in the 1930's

D. Civil Rights legislation of the 1930's

27. Which of the following best describes Clovis people?

A. The earliest Visigoth tribe in Northern Europe

B. The first established culture of the Americas; their first settlements are over 11,000 years old

C. The decedents of King Clovis, Frankish King of the 5th and 6th century

D. An Australian aboriginal group comprised of over 250 distinct languages

Use the map below to answer the question that follows:

28. The lines on the above map represent:

A. Paths of European explores in the 14th century

B. The progression of glaciers in sub Saharan Africa cir 100,000 BCE

C. Trade routes of preliterate African societies

D. The migration of Bantu speaking peoples

29. U.S.-Japanese relations before the start of World War II can best be described as:

A. Peaceful. Both countries interacted largely through corporate interests

B. Increasingly hostile. The U.S. government used economic pressure to stem the rise of Japanese militarism

C. Friendly. The two counties shared common interests in the Pacific and worked together to achieve these ends

D. Hostile. Racism and covert operations undermined any attempt at diplomacy

30. Unlike the U.S. Constitution, the Articles of Confederation:

A. Created a judicial system of inferior courts and a supreme court

B. Established rule by the collective agreement of independent states

C. Called for a large standing army

D. Gave the national government the authority to declare war, coin money, and develop western lands

31. Pre-historic animism can best be described as:

A. A belief that an animating spirit pervades not only sentiment begins, but all material found in nature

B. A central tenant of paganism that places animals on the same spiritual plain as humans

C. An organizational principle that favors the unanimous opinion of the majority over individual self interest

D. The transfer of human qualities into artistic representations on inanimate objects

32. Which of the following best describes the state of American immigration at the turn of the 20th century?

A. Most immigrants settled in rural areas, choosing to pursue occupations similar to those from their homelands

B. Immigrants valued community and settled in areas already populated with members of their own ethnic group

C. A vast majority of married female immigrants worked outside the home in the service or manufacturing industries

D. Immigrants choosing to live in urban environments did so because of their desire to shed the language, habits, and religions of their native homes

Use the following excerpt from Article 22 of the "Covenant of the League of Nations" to answer the four questions that follow.

To those colonies and territories which as a consequence of the late war have ceased to be under the sovereignty of the States which formerly governed them and which are inhabited by peoples not yet able to stand by themselves under the strenuous conditions of the modern world, there should be applied the principle that the well-being and development of such peoples form a sacred trust of civilization and that securities for the performance of this trust should be embodied in this Covenant. The best method of giving practical effect to this principle is that the tutelage of such peoples should be entrusted to advanced nations who by reason of their resources, their experience or their geographical position can best undertake this responsibility, and who are willing to accept it, and that this tutelage should be exercised by them as Mandatories on behalf of the League.

The character of the mandate must differ according to the stage of the development of the people, the geographical situation of the territory, its economic conditions, and other similar circumstances. Certain communities formerly belonging to the Turkish Empire have reached a stage of development where their existence as independent nations can be provisionally recognized subject to the rendering of administrative advice and assistance by a Mandatory until such time as they are able to stand alone. The wishes of these communities must be a principal consideration in the selection of the Mandatory. Other peoples, especially those of Central Africa, are at such a stage that the Mandatory must be responsible for the administration of the territory under conditions which will guarantee freedom of conscience and religion, subject only to the maintenance of public order and morals, the prohibition of abuses such as the slave trade, the arms traffic, and the liquor traffic, and the prevention of the establishment of fortifications or military and naval bases and of military training of the natives for other than police purposes and the defense of territory, and will also secure equal opportunities for the trade and commerce of other Members of the League.

There are territories, such as South-West Africa and certain of the South Pacific Islands, which, owing to the sparseness of their population, or their small size, or their remoteness from the centers of civilization, or their geographical contiguity to the territory of the Mandatory, and other circumstances, can be best administered under the laws of the Mandatory as integral portions of its territory, subject to the safeguards above mentioned in the interests of the indigenous population.

33. What was this document written in response to?

A. The revolutions of the mid-nineteenth century.

B. World War I

C. World War II

D. The build up of tensions during the Cold War

34. What was the primary duty of "Mandatories," as stated in the above?

A. To join together in a peaceful military alliance.

B. To defend the cause of religious liberty.

C. To look after newly created territories.

D. To safeguard democracy in a new world order.

35. Compared to Turkey, the governance of Southwest Africa needed to be:

A. Regulated by the laws of a specific Mandatory nation.

B. More cognizant of religious differences.

C. Ruled by indigenous peoples.

D. Left to develop its own internal structure, without the interference of Mandatories.

36. The above is a useful example of:

A. Social Darwinism in the early twentieth century.

B. Proto-nationalism in the late nineteenth century.

C. Isolationism in the late nineteenth century.

D. Ethnocentrism of the early twentieth century.

37. From the 5th Century BCE to the 9th Century CE, the city of Alexandria in Egypt was politically important because of:

A. Its famed lighthouse

B. Its grain exports

C. Its proximity to the Aegean Sea

D. Its holy temples

38. Which of the following best explains the results of Mao Zedong's "Great Leap Forward"?

A. It propelled an already expanding economy

B. China's working class entered a period of sustained prosperity

C. It produced widespread famines

D. A technology industry now dominated Chinese production

39. The creation of the Federal Bureau of Investigation was prompted by:

A. Fear of Communist conspiracies

B. Gang violence in Chicago

C. The high-profile kidnapping case of baby Lindberg

D. Public outrage over the assassination of President William McKinley by radical bolshevists

40. Which of the following best describes the rational behind the construction of the Panama Canal?

A. To more evenly balance U.S. imports and exports

B. To expand U.S. dominion over the western hemisphere

C. It was to act as U.S. military base for mission to the South Pacific

D. As the first ever joint venture between Central American Countries, the construction project was meant to establish unity

Use the excerpt below from Alfred Thayer Mahan's The Influence of Sea Power on History (1890) to answer the two questions that follow.

. . . [Ho]me trade is but a part of the business of a country bordering on the sea. Foreign necessaries or luxuries must be brought to its ports, either in its own or in foreign ships, which will return, bearing in exchange the products of the country, whether they be the fruits of the earth or the works of men's hands; and it is the wish of every nation that this shipping business should be done by its own vessels.
The ships that thus sail to and fro must have secure ports to which to return, and must, as far as possible, be followed by the protection of their country throughout the voyage. This protection in time of war must be extended by armed shipping. The necessity of a navy, in the restricted sense of the word, springs, therefore, from the existence of a peaceful shipping, and disappears with it, except in the case of a nation which has aggressive tendencies, and keeps up a navy merely as a branch of the military establishment. As the United States has at present no aggressive purposes, and as its merchant service has disappeared, the dwindling of the armed fleet and general lack of interest in it are strictly logical consequences.

41. What, according to Alfred Thayer Mahan, was the ultimate purpose of the American navy?

    A. To protect America's territorial possessions overseas.

    B. To promote and maintain peace with other countries.

    C. To defend America's coastal cities.

    D. To provide safe conduct to merchant vessels and promote American commerce.

42. What larger historical movement does the above passage help explain?

    A. The rise of American industrial power.

    B. The influence of European wars on the American consciousness.

    C. The imperial desires of turn-of-the-century Americans

    D. Hopes for a peaceful, one-world government.

43. Which of the following best describes U.S.-French relations in the 1790s?

A. The enthusiastic support of Jeffersonian Republicans for the French Revolution disintegrated when the revolt grew increasingly more violent.

B. Federalist support of Great Britain ensured that Francophilia (e.g. the love of the French people) would remain at low ebb.

C. A series of presidents sought to build exclusive trade alliances with the French in order to punish British merchants.

D. The balance of U.S.-French relations was determined in large part by the pace of the Napoleonic Wars.

44. Which of the following best describes benevolent societies, temperance organizations, and trade unions of the late nineteenth century?

A. They offered women the opportunity to participate in politics

B. Most were of little real assistance to immigrants, women, or day laborers

C. Women and minorities were largely excluded from participation

D. The Federal Government saw them as inherently seditious and sought to curb their membership

45. All of the following were aspects of the conservative-backed "Contract with America" except:

A. A pledge to lower taxes

B. Guaranteed cuts to welfare

C. A promise to cut military spending

D. A commitment to reducing government waste

46. Before the 1840s, the fastest and the most affordable means of transporting goods inland was:

A. Interstate roads

B. Railroads

C. Canals

D. On horseback

47. In the Roman Republic, religion was:

A. Individualistic

B. Pluralistic

C. Monotheistic

D. Focused on the worship of god-kings

48. In America, child-labor laws were a product of:

A. The Progressive era

B. The Gilded age

C. The Era of Good Feelings

D. The Early Republic

49. Which of the following best describes the immediate impact of the Erie Canal?

A. Bonds issued by the Federal Government covered the costs of construction but also strengthened the Bank of the United States.

B. The canal increased the population of Syracuse, Buffalo, and other western towns.

C. The canal directly contributed to the deterioration of the New York's relationship with Southern states.

D. The canal inspired a canal-building craze in the mid-Atlantic

50. Which of the following was not part of President Theodore Roosevelt's progressive agenda:

A. Support of equal rights for African Americans

B. Calls for the regulation of food and medicine

C. Conservation of American resources

D. Regulation of railroad shipping rates

51. What was John Brown's raid on Harper's Ferry meant to accomplish?

A. Brown was a New England radical who believed the raid would win him popular support.

B. Brown expected to lead the massive slave uprising that he believed was certain to follow.

C. The raid was really nothing more than an attempt to exact revenge for fallen comrades.

D. Brown hoped news of his raid would inspire a series of small-scale slave uprisings throughout the South.

52. How did the television most impact America in the decades following World War II?

A. It led to decreased church attendance and religious affiliation

B. It contributed to growing class distinctions

C. It reinvigorated a flagging home elections industry

D. It helped create a more unified national culture

Use the following excerpt from Thomas Jefferson's Notes on the State of Virginia (1785) to answer the two questions that follow.

In Europe the lands are either cultivated, or locked up against the cultivator. Manufacture must therefore be resorted to of necessity not of choice, to support the surplus of their people. But we have an immensity of land courting the industry of the husbandman. Is it best then that all our citizens should be employed in its improvement, or that one half should be called off from that to exercise manufactures and handicraft arts for the other? Those who labor in the earth are the chosen people of God, if ever he had a chosen people, whose breasts he has made his peculiar deposit for substantial and genuine virtue. It is the focus in which he keeps alive that sacred fire, which otherwise might escape from the face of the earth. Corruption of morals in the mass of cultivators is a phenomenon of which no age nor nation has furnished an example. 'It is the mark set on those, who not looking up to heaven, to their own soil and industry, as does the husbandman, for their sustenance, depend for tt on the casualties and caprice of customers. Dependence begets subservience and venality, suffocates the germ of virtue, and prepares fit tools for the designs of ambition.

This, the natural progress and consequence of the arts, has sometimes perhaps been retarded by accidental circumstances: but, generally speaking, the proportion which the aggregate of the other classes of citizens bears in any state to that of its husbandmen, is the proportion of its unsound to its healthy parts, and is a good-enough barometer whereby to measure its degree of corruption. While we have land to labor then, let us never wish to see our citizens occupied at a work- bench, or twirling a distaff. Carpenters, masons, smiths, are wanting in husbandry: but, for the general operations of manufacture, let our work-shops remain in Europe. It is better to carry provisions and materials to workmen there, than bring them to the provisions and materials, and with them their manners and principles. The loss by the transportation of commodities across the Atlantic will be made up in happiness and permanence of government. The mobs of great cities add just so much to the support of pure government, as sores do to the strength of the human body. It is the manners and spirit of a people which preserve a republic in vigor.

53. Which of the following best describes Jefferson's argument?

A. The plight of the poor farmer shows a weakness in the democratic system.

B. Agricultural, not industrial improvement will ensure the health of the republic.

C. Wealthy industrial tycoons have syphoned off the bulk of the profits and left farmers without hope.

D. Farmers are prone to corruption and therefore in need of government supervision.

54. What, according to Jefferson, is the problem with relying on foreign goods?

A. Domestic producers have a difficult time competing.

D. Foreign luxuries lead to foreign political influences.

C. A reliance on foreign products removes people from a dependence on God.

D. They create mass unemployment in America's cities.

55. In the uprising of German peasants known as the "Peasants War," Martin Luther sided with:

A. German peasants and peasant farmers.

B. German nobility and princes.

C. The Pope in Rome.

D. Cathars, a heretical sect.

56. What qualities best describe members of the Southern Confederacy at the start of the Civil War?

A. Citizens were split over the issue of slavery; many whites disagreed with the institution and wanted to bring it to an end.

B. A great feeling of unanimity and "sameness" prevailed in the South. Southern pride bound previously uncooperative parties together.

C. Southerners were largely in favor of succession but many maintained a strict opposition to any form of central authority, Southern Confederacy or Northern.

D. Opinions varied from state to state, Southerners disagreed about nearly every facet of their new government.

57. The discovery of a Northwest Passage to Asia was the primary goal of early:

A. Portuguese Explorers

B. Spanish Explorers

C. Northern European Explorers

D. Italian Explorers

58. Which of the following best describes the effects of the "little Ice Age", a period that stretched from the 16th to 19th Centuries?

A. It increased the spread of plague-bearing rats throughout northern Europe

B. The population of western Europe declined significantly

C. Summers were longer, winters shorter

D. Western Europe saw its first Monsoons in recorded history

59. Giant stone heads carved by members of the Olmec civilization are thought to be:

A. Astrological symbols

B. Representations of rulers

C. Platforms for human sacrifice

D. Markers of territorial boundaries

Use the following from Andrew Carnegie's *Gospel of Wealth* (1889) to answer the four questions that follow.

The problem of our age is the proper administration of wealth, that the ties of brotherhood may still bind together the rich and poor in harmonious relationship. The conditions of human life have not only been changed, but revolutionized, within the past few hundred years. In former days there was little difference between the dwelling, dress, food, and environment of the chief and those of his retainers. The Indians are to-day where civilized man then was. When visiting the Sioux, I was led to the wigwam of the chief. It was like the others in external appearance, and even within the difference was trifling between it and those of the poorest of his braves. The contrast between the palace of the millionaire and the cottage of the laborer with us to-day measures the change which has come with civilization.

This change, however, is not to be deplored, but welcomed as highly beneficial. It is well, nay, essential, for the progress of the race that the houses of some should be homes for all that is highest and best in literature and the arts, and for all the refinements of civilization, rather than that none should be so. Much better this great irregularity than universal squalor. Without wealth there can be no Maecenas. The "good old times" were not good old times. Neither master nor servant was as well situated then as to-day. A relapse to old conditions would be disastrous to both — not the least so to him who serves — and would sweep away civilization with it. But whether the change be for good or ill, it is upon us, beyond our power to alter, and, therefore, to be accepted and made the best of. It is a waste of time to criticize the inevitable.

The inevitable result of such a mode of manufacture was crude articles at high prices. To-day the world obtains commodities of excellent quality at prices which even the preceding generation would have deemed incredible. In the commercial world similar causes have produced similar results, and the race is benefited thereby. The poor enjoy what the rich could not before afford. What were luxuries have become the necessaries of life. The laborer has now more comforts than the farmer had a few generations ago. The farmer has more luxuries than the landlord had, and is more richly clad and better housed. The landlord has books and pictures rarer and appointments more artistic than the king could then obtain. . . .
Poor and restricted are our opportunities in this life, narrow our horizon, our best work most imperfect; but rich men should be thankful for one inestimable boon. They have it in their power during their lives to busy themselves in organizing benefactions from which the masses of their fellows will derive lasting advantage, and thus dignify their own lives. . . . This, then, is held to be the duty of the man of wealth: To set an example of modest, unostentatious living, shunning display or extravagance; to provide moderately for the legitimate wants of those dependent upon him; and, after doing so, to consider all surplus revenues which come to him simply as trust funds, which he is called upon to administer, and strictly bound as a matter of duty to administer in the manner which, in his judgment, is best calculated to produce the most beneficial results for the community — the man of wealth thus becoming the mere trustee and agent for his poorer brethren, bringing to their service his superior wisdom, experience, and ability to administer, doing for them better than they would or could do for themselves.

60. What was Carnegie's main purpose in writing the above?

A. He was arguing for a redistribution of wealth.

B. He claimed that society operated more efficiently when wealth resided in the hands of only a few.

C. He was praising the modern system of commercial enterprise.

D. He was arguing against those who wanted to raise taxes on the wealthy.

61. Which of the following best describes Carnegie's understanding of pre-industrial society?

A. Workers had more freedom to move from one job to the next.

B. Government worked alongside business to grow the economy.

C. Prices were lower and the goods were of substantially higher quality.

D. There was more social and political equality but the standard of living was much less.

62. What, according to Carnegie, are the responsibilities of the wealthy?

A. They should use their superior wealth and intelligence to look after the poor.

B. The rich must create generational wealth, passing their fortunes on to their sons and daughters.

C. The wealthy should seek to influence the government for the betterment of society.

D. It is the responsibility of the wealthy to strengthen America's standing overseas.

63. Which of the following arguments makes the best historical use of the above passage?

A. A work in defense of government deregulation, citing Carnegie as an example of benevolent wealth.

B. An argument that places Carnegie opposite Marx and compares their similarities and differences.

C. A paraphrased summary, written in a modern vernacular.

D. A narrative history of American philanthropy.

64. How did King James II's attempt to isolate New England radicals in 1777?

A. He placed British garrisons in every major New England town.

B. He pressed for the passage of the "Navigation Acts," a set of laws that placed tight restrictions of New England merchants.

C. He placed pro-British advertisements in most major newspapers of New England.

D. He organized the colonies of New England into a single, unified political entity

65. Which of the following best describes imperial attitudes towards trade and competition in the 15th thru 18th centuries?

A. A positive balance of trade was desirable because it increased military security

B. Tariff-free trade prompted expansion and equal opportunity

C. Competition was restricted so that wars between rival countries are less frequent

D. Government were best when they interfered the least

66. The Mason-Dixon line is a survey boundary between which American states?

A. Maryland and Virginia

B. Washington D.C. and Virginia

C. Pennsylvania and Maryland

D. New York and New Jersey

67. Compared with early Egyptian patriarchy, Mesopotamian patriarchy:

A. Had less of an influence of women

B. Was more persistent and restrictive toward women

C. Had a greater influence of ideas of power and authority

D. Was almost unknown

68. African slaves retained a unique culture that included all of the following, except:

A. A language that mixed English with African dialects

B. Agricultural techniques

C. A stratified system of social hierarchy

D. Religion

Use the excerpt below from President Andrew Jackson's second address before Congress in 1830 to answer the three questions that follow.

It gives me pleasure to announce to Congress that the benevolent policy of the government, steadily pursued for nearly thirty years, in relation to the removal of the Indians beyond the white settlements is approaching to a happy consummation. The consequences of a speedy removal will be important to the United States, to individual states, and to the Indians themselves. The pecuniary advantages which it promises to the government are the least of its recommendations. It puts an end to all possible danger of collision between the authorities of the general and state governments on account of the Indians.
It will separate the Indians from immediate contact with settlements of whites; free them from the power of the states; enable them to pursue happiness in their own way and under their own rude institutions; will retard the progress of decay, which is lessening their numbers, and perhaps cause them gradually, under the protection of the government and through the influence of good counsels, to cast off their savage habits and become an interesting, civilized, and Christian community.

69. Jackson's remarks in this passage can be best described as:

A. Somewhat paternalistic; Indian civilization required careful government oversight.

B. Hostile and indifferent to the way his policies were to be carried out.

C. Remorseful but resigned to his policy.

D. More interested with economic factors than humanitarian considerations.

70. What were the long-term implications of Jackson's policy?

A. The Indian Wars were fought primarily because of its inherent contradictions.

B. It gave a rational for subsequent interactions with Indians.

C. Americans restricted their movement into Indian Territory but their move west brought them into repeated conflict.

D. Westward expansion was slowed because of Jackson's attempts to pacify land-hungry whites.

71. What is the irony of Jackson's reasoning?

A. Separating Indians from whites will help them develop an appreciation for American customs.

B. Removing Indians from their tribal homes will help them establish a greater sense of identity.

C. The "pecuniary advantages" which Indian removal would supposedly bring to the government really only benefited individual settlers.

D. Indian culture was tied directly to kinship networks, not tribal lands.

Read the following excerpt from Thomas Hobbes' *Leviathan* (1651) to answer the two questions that follow:

The difference between these three kinds of Commonwealth [monarchy, democracy, aristocracy] consists not in the difference of power, but in the difference of convenience or aptitude to produce the peace and security of the people; for which end they were instituted. And to compare monarchy with the other two, we may observe: first, that whosoever beareth the person of the people, or is one of that assembly that bears it, beareth also his own natural person. And though he be careful in his politic person to procure the common interest, yet he is more, or no less, careful to procure the private good of himself, his family, kindred and friends; and for the most part, if the public interest chance to cross the private, he prefers the private: for the passions of men are commonly more potent than their reason. From whence it follows that where the public and private interest are most closely united, there is the public most advanced. Now in monarchy the private interest is the same with the public. The riches, power, and honour of a monarch arise only from the riches, strength, and reputation of his subjects. For no king can be rich, nor glorious, nor secure, whose subjects are either poor, or contemptible, or too weak through want, or dissension, to maintain a war against their enemies; whereas in a democracy, or aristocracy, the public prosperity confers not so much to the private fortune of one that is corrupt, or ambitious, as doth many times a perfidious advice, a treacherous action, or a civil war.

72. What, according to Hobbes, is the most effective form of government?

A. Monarchy

B. Democracy

C. Aristocracy

D. Anarchy

73. From where does the monarch derive his/her "riches, power, and honour"?

A. Military victories.

B. The will of the public.

C. Economic policies.

D. The approval of wealthy citizens.

74. Early 19th century proposals for a national system of roads and turnpikes in America were inspired by:

A. The high costs of overland shipping

B. The need to transport soldiers and military equipment to the far reaches of the frontier.

C. An improved relationship with the British government and the desire to enhance trade

D. The discovery of oil in western Pennsylvania.

75. Which of the following most directly contributed to America's economic decline following the War of 1812?

A. British Corn Laws.

B. French shipping embargoes.

C. The increased price of British goods shipped to American ports

D. New limited liability business arrangements

76. "Lend-Lease" was an attempt to:

A. Further isolate the United States from the war in Europe

B. Promote American manufacturing through direct government assistance

C. Provide American farmers with credit during a particularly bad growing season

D. Strengthen the Allied cause without formally committing U.S. military forces

77. Unlike early proponents of mercantilism, Adam Smith emphasized the:

A. Importance for government intervention in commercial endeavors

B. Necessity of safeguarding human welfare

C. Invisible hand in the maintenance of free market

D. Zero sum game of European powers

78. Which of the following best explains the beliefs and practices of the Flagellants?

A. They were Christian polytheists, believing in a god of darkness and a god of light.

B. They believed that by beating themselves with leather straps, God would bring an end to the plague.

C. They were a mendicant (begging) order and sought lives of Christian purity by living as Christ's disciples.

D. They were the Catholic Church's first teaching order, establishing schools and codifying languages in order to transmit the Christian doctrine.

79. Native American resistance to the U.S. Government, in the so called "Indian Wars" of the 1860s and 1870s, ultimately failed because of:

A. Trade restrictions against Indian nations

B. The technological advantages of the U.S. Army

C. Canadian Military assistance on the western frontier

D. War weariness among Native American warriors

80. World War II influenced all aspects of American society, but this was the most dramatic legacy of the war:

A. A permanent change in racial attitudes

B. A greatly expanded role for women in the workplace

C. The dramatic increase in the size of the Federal government

D. The creation of an American class system

81. Which of the following best describes Abraham Lincoln's reasons for suspending habeas corpus in the early months of the civil war?

A. It gave Lincoln the legal authority to treat American citizens as enemy combatants

B. It imposed martial law on politically unstable areas of the North

C. It gave union generals the authority to arrest and detain those who interfered with or acted against union troops

D. It allowed him to silence political rivals and those who openly criticized the Federal Government

Use the following sayings attributed to Confucius (Cir. 551–479 BC) to answer the three questions that follow.

The Master said: In ruling a country of a thousand chariots there should be scrupulous attention to business, honesty, economy, charity, and employment of the people at the proper season. A virtuous ruler is like the Pole-star, which keeps its place, while all the other stars do homage to it. People despotically governed and kept in order by punishments may avoid infraction of the law, but they will lose their moral sense. People virtuously governed and kept in order by the inner law of self-control will retain their moral sense, and moreover become good.

The Master said: If a country had none by good rulers for a hundred years, crime might be stamped out and the death-penalty abolished. How true theis saying is! If a kingly sovereign were to appear, by the end of one generation natural goodness would prevail. If a man can reform his own heart, what should hinder him from taking part in government? But if he cannot reform his own heart, what has he to do with reforming others?

At home, a young man should show the qualities of a son; abroad, those of a younger brother. He should be circumspect but truthful. He should have charity in his heart for all men, but associate only with the virtuous. After thus regulating his conduct, his surplus energy should be devoted to literary culture.
In the matter of food and lodging, the nobler type of man does not seek mere repletion and comfort. He is earnest in his affairs and cautious in his speech, and frequents virtuous company for his own improvement. He may be called one truly bent on the study of virtue.

82. Which of the following best describes Confucius' philosophy of leadership?

A. Lead by force, crush opposition and inspire fear whenever possible.

B. The enlightened ruler is he who places the many over the few and holds himself up to public criticism.

C. None can judge the ruler but himself.

D. Government works best when it works the least. Excessive laws harm the morality of the people.

83. How could you characterize the author's intentions behind this passage?

A. It is a religious text meant to inspire devotion to a single deity or pantheon of deities.

B. It is a type of legal code that the author hopes will form the moral law of the land.

C. There is no specific reason given for these sayings; we should live lives of self-control and morality simply because it is good.

D. By stressing virtue and moral leadership the author is calling for rulers to lighten oppressive legal burdens, taxes, laws, prisons, etc.

84. What could this document reveal about historical change?

A. The emphasis on strong moral leadership could suggest a decline in governmental authority and uncertainty among the people.

B. The focus on personal duty and responsibility leads us to believe that Chinese authority of the sixth and fifth centuries BCE was gaining strength and solidifying into a strong regional power.

C. By drawing attention to duties "abroad" we see the expansion of Chinese influence in foreign countries.

D. His emphasis on learning and wisdom could reflect a larger trend towards state-sponsored education.

85. Which of the following most directly contributed to increasing disparities between the wealthiest and poorest Americans in the 1980s?

A. Tax breaks to members of the middle class undermined supply-side economic theory

B. Government-sponsored social welfare programs increased dramatically throughout the decade

C. Military spending reached all time highs in 1986

D. Most new jobs were in low-paid service positions

86. "Green backs" issued by the Federal Government were proposed as a means to:

A. Finance mounting war debts

B. End rising unemployment

C. Facilitate the growth and stability of the Bank of the United States

D. Promote U.S. business interests over foreign competitors

87. Unlike the earliest civilizations of the middle east, Central America, or China, the peoples of the Indus River Valley appear to have:

A. Enjoyed thousands of years of peace and prosperity

B. Lacked an organized political hierarchy

C. Lived in isolation from the rest of the world

D. Developed a symbolic alphabet

88. The election of 1876 resulted in which of the following Republican concessions?

A. A constitutional amendment that guaranteed African Americans separate but equal legal status

B. Financial assistance in excess of $100 million dollars to aid southern reconstruction

C. An agreement to withdraw federal troops from Southern states

D. The Vice President would be chosen from Democratic party

Use this extract from St. Ignatius of Loyola's *Spiritual Exercises* (cir. 1522) to answer the three questions that follow:

Let the following Rules be observed.

First Rule. The first: All judgment laid aside, we ought to have our mind ready and prompt to obey, in all, the true Spouse of Christ our Lord, which is our holy Mother the Church Hierarchical.

Second Rule. The second: To praise confession to a Priest, and the reception of the most Holy Sacrament of the Altar once in the year, and much more each month, and much better from week to week, with the conditions required and due.

Fifth Rule. The fifth: To praise vows of Religion, of obedience, of poverty, of chastity and of other perfections of supererogation. And it is to be noted that as the vow is about the things which approach to Evangelical perfection, a vow ought not to be made in the things which withdraw from it, such as to be a merchant, or to be married, etc.

Sixth Rule. To praise relics of the Saints, giving veneration to them and praying to the Saints; and to praise Stations, pilgrimages, Indulgences, pardons, Cruzadas, and candles lighted in the churches.

Eighth Rule. To praise the ornaments and the buildings of churches; likewise images, and to venerate them according to what they represent.

Ninth Rule. Finally, to praise all precepts of the Church, keeping the mind prompt to find reasons in their 'defence and in no manner against them.

89. What can this excerpt tell us about Loyola's religious ideals?

   A. He believed that all of the traditional Catholic rites and sacraments were legitimate, except the sale of indulgences.

   B. He believed that Roman Catholics could be spiritual (i.e. evangelical) but still hold fast to the teachings of the Church.

   C. This work exposes a growing rift between the papacy and members of the mendicant (begging) orders.

   D. Loyola was mainly interested in restoring the authority of local priests, building them up against the wishes of the Pope.

90. This passage is a prime example of:

   A. Christian humanism

   B. Religious secularism

   C. Spiritual pluralism

   D. Spiritual influences inspired by the scientific revolution.

91. What does movement is this document most relevant to?

   A. The Catholic Reformation

   B. The Protestant Reformation

   C. The investiture controversy.

   D. The Spanish Inquisition

Read the following excerpt from Charlemagne's *Capitulary on Saxony* (785) to answer the three questions that follow.

1. It was pleasing to all that the churches of Christ, which are now being built in Saxony and consecrated to God, should not have less, but greater and more illustrious honor, than the fanes of the idols had had.

3. If any one shall have entered a church by violence and shall have carried off anything in it by force or theft, or shall have burned the church itself, let him be punished by death.

5. If any one shall have killed a bishop or priest or deacon, let him likewise be punished capitally.

6. If any one deceived by the devil shall have believed, after the manner of the pagans, that any man or woman is a witch and eats men, and on this account shall have burned the person, or shall have given the person's flesh to others to eat, or shall have eaten it himself, let him be punished by a capital sentence.

7. If any one, in accordance with pagan rites, shall have caused the body of a dead man to be burned and shall have reduced his bones to ashes, let him be punished capitally.

8. If any one of the race of the Saxons hereafter concealed among them shall have wished to hide himself unbaptized, and shall have scorned to come to baptism and shall have wished to remain a pagan, let him be punished by death.

9. If any one shall have sacrificed a man to the devil, and after the manner of the pagans shall have presented him as a victim to the demons, let him be punished by death.

10. If any one shall have formed a conspiracy with the pagans against the Christians, or shall have wished to join with them in opposition to the Christians, let him be punished by death; and whosoever shall have consented to this same fraudulently against the king and the Christian people, let him be punished by death.

17. Likewise, in accordance with the mandate of God, we command that all shall give a tithe of their property and labor to the churches and priests; let the nobles as well as the freemen, and likewise the lilt, according to that which God shall have given to each Christian, return a part to God.

18. That on the Lord's day no meetings and public judicial assemblages shall be held, unless perchance in a case of great necessity or when war compels it, but all shall go to the church to hear the word of God, and shall be free for prayers or good works. Likewise, also, on the especial festivals they shall devote themselves to God and to the services of the church, and shall refrain from secular assemblies.

92. Which of the following best describes Charlemagne's attitude toward non-Christians?

   A. He had little tolerance for dissenters.

   B. Religious differences were respected and upheld by law.

   C. He struck a middle ground with those opposed to Christianity, laws were based on Christian doctrine but most were free to choose what religion they practiced.

   D. The most severe punishments were reserved for those who disrespected the authority of the king.

93. How does this excerpt demonstrate Charlemagne's obligations to the Christian Church?

   A. It shows that his primary responsibility was to protect the boarder between Christians and pagan barbarians.

   B. It demonstrates his desire to promote the interests of the Pope in Rome.

   C. It provides a rational behind the forced conversions of the Franks.

   D. It shows that he saw himself as a Christian king, with a mandate to rule Christians, and only Christians.

94. The above shows that Charlemagne's Christian policies were met with:

   A. Widespread acceptance by non-Christian Saxons.

   B. Resistance from only the poorer classes of Saxons.

   C. Objections by all classes of Saxon society.

   D. Anger from the Frankish people.

95. Which of the following best describes the “spoils system” under President Ulysses S. Grant?

A. The North’s right to gather and then re-divide and sell southern property seized during the Civil War

B. The Federal Government’s absolute right to profits generated by trade tariffs

C. A climate of corruption, bribery, and graft that extended from the Executive office through all levels of government

D. The systematic removal and relocation of Native Americans from tribal lands and the sale of these lands to government favorites

96. The adoption of the horse by Plains Indians enhanced their:

A. Political and territorial independence

B. Speed and efficiency in hunting

C. Trade relations with Western Anglos

D. Trust and reverence for White Settlers

97. Jefferson Davis demanded an immediate withdraw of Federal troops from Fort Sumter because their presence:

A. Deterred ships from entering Charleston harbor

B. Undermined the confidence of several confederate states

C. Promoted rebellion among the slaves of Charleston

D. Insulted the pride of Southerners

98. Cuneiform writing was initially used for:

A. Religious rites

B. Royal decrees

C. Predictions of future events

D. Inventories of merchandise

Use the following excerpt adapted from *The Journey of William of Rubruck* (cir. 1255) to answer the two questions that follow.

The matrons make for themselves most beautiful (luggage) carts. . . . A single rich Tartar has one or two-hundred such carts with coffers. Baatu, the grandson of Genghis Khan, has twenty-six wives, each of whom has a large dwelling, exclusive of the other little ones which they set up after the big one, and which are like closets, in which the sewing girls live, and to each of these (large) dwellings are attached two carts. And when they set up their houses, the first wife places her dwelling on the extreme west side, and after her the others according to their rank, so that the last wife will be in the extreme east; and there will be the distance of a stone's throw between the house of one wife and that of another. The home of a rich Moal seems like a large town, though there will be very few men in it. One girl will lead twenty or thirty carts, for the country is flat, and they link the ox or camel carts the one after the other, and a girl will sit on the front one driving the ox, and all the others follow after with the same gait.

When they have fixed their dwelling, with the main door facing south, they set up the couch of the master on the north side. The side for the women is always the east side, that is to say, on the left of the house of the master, he sitting on his couch with his face turned to the south. The side for the men is the west side, that is, on the right. Men coming into the house would never hang up their bows on the side of the women. And over the head of the master is always an image of felt, like a doll or statuette, which they call the brother of the master; another similar one is above the head of the mistress, which they call the brother of the mistress, and they are attached to the wall; and higher up between the two of them is one, who is, as it were, the guardian of the whole dwelling. The mistress places in her house on her right side, in a conspicuous place at the foot of her couch, a goat-skin full of wool or other stuff, and beside it a very little statuette looking in the direction of the attendants and women. Beside the entry on the women's side is yet another image, with a cow's tit for the women, who milk the cows; for it is part of the duty of the women to milk the cows. On the other side of the entry, toward the men, is another statue with a mare's tit for the men who milk the mares.

99. The use of this source by historians might be complicated by:

A. The author's attempt to link foreign practices with behaviors of his own people.

B. A lack of empathy for women. The author provides gendered descriptions of all work obligations.

C. A failure to understand the religious practices of these people.

D. The author's perspective; he was probably treated very well during his stay and shown only the best qualities of the people.

100. Which of the following best describes the values of this culture?

A. The love of children and family trump all other concerns.

B. War and heroic feats of honor distinguish the value of one man from another.

C. Females have a relatively high standing despite their obvious subornation to men.

D. Religion dominates their lives and guides all their decisions.

Answer Keys

Exam 1 Answer Key

1.	B	U.S. HISTORY ERAS 1-3: PREHISTORIC AMERICA TO 1800 CE
2.	B	U.S. HISTORY ERAS 1-3: PREHISTORIC AMERICA TO 1800 CE
3.	C	U.S. HISTORY ERAS 1-3: PREHISTORIC AMERICA TO 1800 CE
4.	D	WORLD HISTORY ERA 5: 300-1500 CE
5.	B	WORLD HISTORY ERA 5: 300-1500 CE
6.	B	WORLD HISTORY ERA 5: 300-1500 CE
7.	B	U.S. HISTORY ERA 8: 1945 TO 1970 CE
8.	A	WORLD HISTORY ERA 4: 1000-300 CE
9.	B	U.S. HISTORY ERA 8: 1945 TO 1970 CE
10.	C	DEMOCRATIC VALUES, CITIZENSHIP, PUBLIC POLICY
11.	A	DEMOCRATIC VALUES, CITIZENSHIP, PUBLIC POLICY
12.	B	WORLD HISTORY ERA 6: 1400-1700 CE
13.	C	HISTORICAL CONCEPTS
14.	C	HISTORICAL CONCEPTS
15.	D	HISTORICAL CONCEPTS
16.	B	GEOGRAPHY: CONCEPTS AND TERMS
17.	C	GEOGRAPHY: RELATIONSHIP WITH HISTORY
18.	A	U.S. HISTORY ERA 9: 1970 TO THE PRESENT
19.	A	U.S. HISTORY ERA 6: 1870 TO 1920 CE
20.	A	U.S. HISTORY ERA 9: 1970 TO THE PRESENT
21.	A	WORLD HISTORY ERAS 1-3: HUMAN SOCIETY TO 4000 BCE TO 300 CE
22.	D	WORLD HISTORY ERAS 1-3: HUMAN SOCIETY TO 4000 BCE TO 300 CE
23.	C	U.S. HISTORY ERA 5: 1850 TO 1877 CE
24.	C	GEOGRAPHY: RELATIONSHIP WITH HISTORY

25.	B	GEOGRAPHY: RELATIONSHIP WITH HISTORY
26.	C	WORLD HISTORY ERAS 1-3: HUMAN SOCIETY TO 4000 BCE TO 300 CE
27.	B	WORLD HISTORY ERA 6: 1400-1700 CE
28.	C	WORLD HISTORY ERA 6: 1400-1700 CE
29.	D	WORLD HISTORY ERA 6: 1400-1700 CE
30.	B	WORLD HISTORY ERAS 1-3: HUMAN SOCIETY TO 4000 BCE TO 300 CE
31.	C	U.S. HISTORY ERA 6: 1870 TO 1920 CE
32.	B	WORLD HISTORY ERA 4: 1000-300 CE
33.	B	U.S. HISTORY ERA 4: 1792 TO 1861 CE
34.	A	WORLD HISTORY ERAS 1-3: HUMAN SOCIETY TO 4000 BCE TO 300 CE
35.	A	DEMOCRATIC VALUES, CITIZENSHIP, PUBLIC POLICY
36.	B	U.S. HISTORY ERA 7: 1920 TO 1945 CE
37.	D	HISTORICAL CONCEPTS
38.	B	HISTORICAL CONCEPTS
39.	C	HISTORICAL CONCEPTS
40.	A	HISTORICAL CONCEPTS
41.	B	HISTORICAL CONCEPTS
42.	A	U.S. HISTORY ERA 6: 1870 TO 1920 CE
43.	C	U.S. HISTORY ERA 6: 1870 TO 1920 CE
44.	D	GEOGRAPHY: CONCEPTS AND TERMS
45.	A	WORLD HISTORY ERAS 1-3: HUMAN SOCIETY TO 4000 BCE TO 300 CE
46.	C	U.S. HISTORY ERA 7: 1920 TO 1945 CE
47.	B	U.S. HISTORY ERA 9: 1970 TO THE PRESENT
48.	D	WORLD HISTORY ERAS 1-3: HUMAN SOCIETY TO 4000 BCE TO 300 CE
49.	C	GEOGRAPHY: RELATIONSHIP WITH HISTORY
50.	B	U.S. HISTORY ERA 9: 1970 TO THE PRESENT

51.	D	WORLD HISTORY ERAS 1-3: HUMAN SOCIETY TO 4000 BCE TO 300 CE
52.	B	ECONOMICS: TERMS, CONCEPTS, RELATIONSHIP WITH HISTORY
53.	B	DEMOCRATIC VALUES, CITIZENSHIP, PUBLIC POLICY
54.	A	U.S. HISTORY ERA 5: 1850 TO 1877 CE
55.	A	U.S. HISTORY ERA 5: 1850 TO 1877 CE
56.	C	U.S. HISTORY ERA 7: 1920 TO 1945 CE
57.	D	WORLD HISTORY ERAS 1-3: HUMAN SOCIETY TO 4000 BCE TO 300 CE
58.	A	WORLD HISTORY ERA 4: 1000-300 CE
59.	D	HISTORICAL CONCEPTS
60.	D	U.S. HISTORY ERA 6: 1870 TO 1920 CE
61.	B	U.S. HISTORY ERA 7: 1920 TO 1945 CE
62.	D	U.S. HISTORY ERA 4: 1792 TO 1861 CE
63.	C	GEOGRAPHY: CONCEPTS AND TERMS
64.	A	U.S. HISTORY ERA 4: 1792 TO 1861 CE
65.	C	HISTORICAL CONCEPTS
66.	A	GEOGRAPHY: CONCEPTS AND TERMS
67.	D	POLITICAL SCIENCE: CONCEPTS AND HISTORICAL CONNECTION
68.	A	U.S. HISTORY ERA 4: 1792 TO 1861 CE
69.	B	U.S. HISTORY ERAS 1-3: PREHISTORIC AMERICA TO 1800 CE
70.	C	HISTORICAL CONCEPTS
71.	D	WORLD HISTORY ERA 5: 300-1500 CE
72.	C	WORLD HISTORY ERA 5: 300-1500 CE
73.	B	DEMOCRATIC VALUES, CITIZENSHIP, PUBLIC POLICY
74.	C	ECONOMICS: TERMS, CONCEPTS, RELATIONSHIP WITH HISTORY
75.	B	U.S. HISTORY ERAS 1-3: PREHISTORIC AMERICA TO 1800 CE
76.	A	U.S. HISTORY ERA 8: 1945 TO 1970 CE

77.	C	ECONOMICS: TERMS, CONCEPTS, RELATIONSHIP WITH HISTORY
78.	B	ECONOMICS: TERMS, CONCEPTS, RELATIONSHIP WITH HISTORY
79.	A	WORLD HISTORY ERAS 1-3: HUMAN SOCIETY TO 4000 BCE TO 300 CE
80.	B	WORLD HISTORY ERAS 1-3: HUMAN SOCIETY TO 4000 BCE TO 300 CE
81.	C	WORLD HISTORY ERAS 1-3: HUMAN SOCIETY TO 4000 BCE TO 300 CE
82.	B	GEOGRAPHY: CONCEPTS AND TERMS
83.	A	WORLD HISTORY ERA 7: 1700-1914 CE
84.	C	U.S. HISTORY ERAS 1-3: PREHISTORIC AMERICA TO 1800 CE
85.	A	POLITICAL SCIENCE: CONCEPTS AND HISTORICAL CONNECTION
86.	D	POLITICAL SCIENCE: CONCEPTS AND HISTORICAL CONNECTION
87.	D	GEOGRAPHY: CONCEPTS AND TERMS
88.	C	ECONOMICS: TERMS, CONCEPTS, RELATIONSHIP WITH HISTORY
89.	A	U.S. HISTORY ERA 5: 1850 TO 1877 CE
90.	A	U.S. HISTORY ERA 7: 1920 TO 1945 CE
91.	B	U.S. HISTORY ERA 8: 1945 TO 1970 CE
92.	C	POLITICAL SCIENCE: CONCEPTS AND HISTORICAL CONNECTION
93.	A	U.S. HISTORY ERA 6: 1870 TO 1920 CE
94.	C	DEMOCRATIC VALUES, CITIZENSHIP, PUBLIC POLICY
95.	C	WORLD HISTORY ERAS 1-3: HUMAN SOCIETY TO 4000 BCE TO 300 CE
96.	A	WORLD HISTORY ERAS 1-3: HUMAN SOCIETY TO 4000 BCE TO 300 CE
97.	C	WORLD HISTORY ERAS 1-3: HUMAN SOCIETY TO 4000 BCE TO 300 CE
98.	C	U.S. HISTORY ERAS 1-3: PREHISTORIC AMERICA TO 1800 CE
99.	A	HISTORICAL CONCEPTS
100.	D	U.S. HISTORY ERAS 1-3: PREHISTORIC AMERICA TO 1800 CE

Exam 2 Answer Key

1.	C	WORLD HISTORY ERA 4: 1000-300 CE
2.	A	U.S. HISTORY ERAS 1-3: PREHISTORIC AMERICA TO 1800 CE
3.	D	GEOGRAPHY: RELATIONSHIP WITH HISTORY
4.	B	GEOGRAPHY: CONCEPTS AND TERMS
5.	B	GEOGRAPHY: CONCEPTS AND TERMS
6.	D	POLITICAL SCIENCE: CONCEPTS AND HISTORICAL CONNECTION
7.	D	POLITICAL SCIENCE: CONCEPTS AND HISTORICAL CONNECTION
8.	A	POLITICAL SCIENCE: CONCEPTS AND HISTORICAL CONNECTION
9.	A	U.S. HISTORY ERA 8: 1945 TO 1970 CE
10.	D	U.S. HISTORY ERA 5: 1850 TO 1877 CE
11.	C	U.S. HISTORY ERA 7: 1920 TO 1945 CE
12.	D	U.S. HISTORY ERAS 1-3: PREHISTORIC AMERICA TO 1800 CE
13.	C	POLITICAL SCIENCE: CONCEPTS AND HISTORICAL CONNECTION
14.	C	POLITICAL SCIENCE: CONCEPTS AND HISTORICAL CONNECTION
15.	D	U.S. HISTORY ERAS 1-3: PREHISTORIC AMERICA TO 1800 CE
16.	D	U.S. HISTORY ERA 4: 1792 TO 1861 CE
17.	B	U.S. HISTORY ERA 4: 1792 TO 1861 CE
18.	B	U.S. HISTORY ERA 4: 1792 TO 1861 CE
19.	C	U.S. HISTORY ERA 9: 1970 TO THE PRESENT
20.	A	U.S. HISTORY ERA 6: 1870 TO 1920 CE
21.	D	WORLD HISTORY ERA 5: 300-1500 CE
22.	D	WORLD HISTORY ERA 5: 300-1500 CE
23.	B	HISTORICAL CONCEPTS
24.	A	HISTORICAL CONCEPTS

25. B DEMOCRATIC VALUES, CITIZENSHIP, PUBLIC POLICY

26. B DEMOCRATIC VALUES, CITIZENSHIP, PUBLIC POLICY

27. A ECONOMICS: TERMS, CONCEPTS, RELATIONSHIP WITH HISTORY

28. C WORLD HISTORY ERAS 1-3: HUMAN SOCIETY TO 4000 BCE TO 300 CE

29. A DEMOCRATIC VALUES, CITIZENSHIP, PUBLIC POLICY

30. C U.S. HISTORY ERA 5: 1850 TO 1877 CE

31. C U.S. HISTORY ERAS 1-3: PREHISTORIC AMERICA TO 1800 CE

32. D WORLD HISTORY ERAS 1-3: HUMAN SOCIETY TO 4000 BCE TO 300 CE

33. A U.S. HISTORY ERA 9: 1970 TO THE PRESENT

34. A ECONOMICS: TERMS, CONCEPTS, RELATIONSHIP WITH HISTORY

35. B WORLD HISTORY ERAS 1-3: HUMAN SOCIETY TO 4000 BCE TO 300 CE

36. A HISTORICAL CONCEPTS

37. A WORLD HISTORY ERA 7: 1700-1914 CE

38. B WORLD HISTORY ERA 7: 1700-1914 CE

39. D U.S. HISTORY ERAS 1-3: PREHISTORIC AMERICA TO 1800 CE

40. D U.S. HISTORY ERA 7: 1920 TO 1945 CE

41. B GEOGRAPHY: CONCEPTS AND TERMS

42. B U.S. HISTORY ERA 5: 1850 TO 1877 CE

43. A WORLD HISTORY ERAS 1-3: HUMAN SOCIETY TO 4000 BCE TO 300 CE

44. C HISTORICAL CONCEPTS

45. B U.S. HISTORY ERA 6: 1870 TO 1920 CE

46. D U.S. HISTORY ERA 6: 1870 TO 1920 CE

47. D U.S. HISTORY ERAS 1-3: PREHISTORIC AMERICA TO 1800 CE

48. A GEOGRAPHY: CONCEPTS AND TERMS

49. D DEMOCRATIC VALUES, CITIZENSHIP, PUBLIC POLICY

50. B WORLD HISTORY ERA 4: 1000-300 CE

51.	B	WORLD HISTORY ERAS 1-3: HUMAN SOCIETY TO 4000 BCE TO 300 CE
52.	B	U.S. HISTORY ERA 8: 1945 TO 1970 CE
53.	B	WORLD HISTORY ERAS 1-3: HUMAN SOCIETY TO 4000 BCE TO 300 CE
54.	D	WORLD HISTORY ERAS 1-3: HUMAN SOCIETY TO 4000 BCE TO 300 CE
55.	C	WORLD HISTORY ERAS 1-3: HUMAN SOCIETY TO 4000 BCE TO 300 CE
56.	A	WORLD HISTORY ERAS 1-3: HUMAN SOCIETY TO 4000 BCE TO 300 CE
57.	A	DEMOCRATIC VALUES, CITIZENSHIP, PUBLIC POLICY
58.	A	GEOGRAPHY: RELATIONSHIP WITH HISTORY
59.	C	U.S. HISTORY ERA 9: 1970 TO THE PRESENT
60.	B	WORLD HISTORY ERAS 1-3: HUMAN SOCIETY TO 4000 BCE TO 300 CE
61.	D	WORLD HISTORY ERAS 1-3: HUMAN SOCIETY TO 4000 BCE TO 300 CE
62.	C	POLITICAL SCIENCE: CONCEPTS AND HISTORICAL CONNECTION
63.	A	U.S. HISTORY ERA 7: 1920 TO 1945 CE
64.	A	GEOGRAPHY: CONCEPTS AND TERMS
65.	B	WORLD HISTORY ERA 5: 300-1500 CE
66.	B	WORLD HISTORY ERA 5: 300-1500 CE
67.	A	HISTORICAL CONCEPTS
68.	D	GEOGRAPHY: CONCEPTS AND TERMS
69.	B	WORLD HISTORY ERAS 1-3: HUMAN SOCIETY TO 4000 BCE TO 300 CE
70.	D	ECONOMICS: TERMS, CONCEPTS, RELATIONSHIP WITH HISTORY
71.	D	DEMOCRATIC VALUES, CITIZENSHIP, PUBLIC POLICY
72.	B	WORLD HISTORY ERA 6: 1400-1700 CE
73.	C	WORLD HISTORY ERA 6: 1400-1700 CE
74.	D	WORLD HISTORY ERA 6: 1400-1700 CE
75.	B	U.S. HISTORY ERA 4: 1792 TO 1861 CE
76.	B	GEOGRAPHY: CONCEPTS AND TERMS

77.	A	U.S. HISTORY ERA 4: 1792 TO 1861 CE
78.	B	U.S. HISTORY ERA 7: 1920 TO 1945 CE
79.	A	DEMOCRATIC VALUES, CITIZENSHIP, PUBLIC POLICY
80.	D	U.S. HISTORY ERA 4: 1792 TO 1861 CE
81.	A	HISTORICAL CONCEPTS
82.	A	WORLD HISTORY ERAS 1-3: HUMAN SOCIETY TO 4000 BCE TO 300 CE
83.	A	U.S. HISTORY ERA 9: 1970 TO THE PRESENT
84.	A	WORLD HISTORY ERAS 1-3: HUMAN SOCIETY TO 4000 BCE TO 300 CE
85.	D	WORLD HISTORY ERA 6: 1400-1700 CE
86.	B	ECONOMICS: TERMS, CONCEPTS, RELATIONSHIP WITH HISTORY
87.	B	U.S. HISTORY ERA 4: 1792 TO 1861 CE
88.	A	WORLD HISTORY ERAS 1-3: HUMAN SOCIETY TO 4000 BCE TO 300 CE
89.	B	WORLD HISTORY ERA 5: 300-1500 CE
90.	A	U.S. HISTORY ERA 4: 1792 TO 1861 CE
91.	D	GEOGRAPHY: CONCEPTS AND TERMS
92.	D	U.S. HISTORY ERA 4: 1792 TO 1861 CE
93.	A	WORLD HISTORY ERA 5: 300-1500 CE
94.	C	U.S. HISTORY ERA 5: 1850 TO 1877 CE
95.	A	HISTORICAL CONCEPTS
96.	B	U.S. HISTORY ERA 8: 1945 TO 1970 CE
97.	B	WORLD HISTORY ERAS 1-3: HUMAN SOCIETY TO 4000 BCE TO 300 CE
98.	A	ECONOMICS: TERMS, CONCEPTS, RELATIONSHIP WITH HISTORY
99.	B	WORLD HISTORY ERAS 1-3: HUMAN SOCIETY TO 4000 BCE TO 300 CE
100.	D	ECONOMICS: TERMS, CONCEPTS, RELATIONSHIP WITH HISTORY

Exam 3 Answer Key

1. C DEMOCRATIC VALUES, CITIZENSHIP, PUBLIC POLICY
2. D GEOGRAPHY: RELATIONSHIP WITH HISTORY
3. D U.S. HISTORY ERAS 1-3: PREHISTORIC AMERICA TO 1800 CE
4. B WORLD HISTORY ERAS 1-3: HUMAN SOCIETY TO 4000 BCE TO 300 CE
5. A ECONOMICS: TERMS, CONCEPTS, RELATIONSHIP WITH HISTORY
6. A WORLD HISTORY ERAS 1-3: HUMAN SOCIETY TO 4000 BCE TO 300 CE
7. A U.S. HISTORY ERA 6: 1870 TO 1920 CE
8. C GEOGRAPHY: RELATIONSHIP WITH HISTORY
9. B GEOGRAPHY: CONCEPTS AND TERMS
10. C HISTORICAL CONCEPTS
11. B WORLD HISTORY ERAS 1-3: HUMAN SOCIETY TO 4000 BCE TO 300 CE
12. A HISTORICAL CONCEPTS
13. A POLITICAL SCIENCE: CONCEPTS AND HISTORICAL CONNECTION
14. A U.S. HISTORY ERAS 1-3: PREHISTORIC AMERICA TO 1800 CE
15. B U.S. HISTORY ERA 7: 1920 TO 1945 CE
16. C U.S. HISTORY ERA 9: 1970 TO THE PRESENT
17. C WORLD HISTORY ERAS 1-3: HUMAN SOCIETY TO 4000 BCE TO 300 CE
18. C HISTORICAL CONCEPTS
19. D HISTORICAL CONCEPTS
20. D WORLD HISTORY ERAS 1-3: HUMAN SOCIETY TO 4000 BCE TO 300 CE
21. D GEOGRAPHY: RELATIONSHIP WITH HISTORY
22. A WORLD HISTORY ERAS 1-3: HUMAN SOCIETY TO 4000 BCE TO 300 CE
23. D U.S. HISTORY ERA 8: 1945 TO 1970 CE
24. B DEMOCRATIC VALUES, CITIZENSHIP, PUBLIC POLICY

25.	C	GEOGRAPHY: RELATIONSHIP WITH HISTORY
26.	A	U.S. HISTORY ERA 7: 1920 TO 1945 CE
27.	B	WORLD HISTORY ERAS 1-3: HUMAN SOCIETY TO 4000 BCE TO 300 CE
28.	D	WORLD HISTORY ERAS 1-3: HUMAN SOCIETY TO 4000 BCE TO 300 CE
29.	B	U.S. HISTORY ERA 7: 1920 TO 1945 CE
30.	B	DEMOCRATIC VALUES, CITIZENSHIP, PUBLIC POLICY
31.	A	WORLD HISTORY ERAS 1-3: HUMAN SOCIETY TO 4000 BCE TO 300 CE
32.	B	U.S. HISTORY ERA 6: 1870 TO 1920 CE
33.	B	WORLD HISTORY ERA 7: 1700-1914 CE
34.	C	WORLD HISTORY ERA 7: 1700-1914 CE
35.	A	WORLD HISTORY ERA 7: 1700-1914 CE
36.	D	HISTORICAL CONCEPTS
37.	B	GEOGRAPHY: RELATIONSHIP WITH HISTORY
38.	C	ECONOMICS: TERMS, CONCEPTS, RELATIONSHIP WITH HISTORY
39.	A	U.S. HISTORY ERA 6: 1870 TO 1920 CE
40.	B	GEOGRAPHY: RELATIONSHIP WITH HISTORY
41.	D	U.S. HISTORY ERA 6: 1870 TO 1920 CE
42.	C	HISTORICAL CONCEPTS
43.	A	U.S. HISTORY ERAS 1-3: PREHISTORIC AMERICA TO 1800 CE
44.	A	U.S. HISTORY ERA 6: 1870 TO 1920 CE
45.	C	U.S. HISTORY ERA 9: 1970 TO THE PRESENT
46.	C	GEOGRAPHY: RELATIONSHIP WITH HISTORY
47.	B	WORLD HISTORY ERAS 1-3: HUMAN SOCIETY TO 4000 BCE TO 300 CE
48.	A	ECONOMICS: TERMS, CONCEPTS, RELATIONSHIP WITH HISTORY
49.	B	U.S. HISTORY ERA 4: 1792 TO 1861 CE
50.	A	U.S. HISTORY ERA 6: 1870 TO 1920 CE

51.	B	U.S. HISTORY ERA 4: 1792 TO 1861 CE
52.	D	U.S. HISTORY ERA 8: 1945 TO 1970 CE
53.	B	U.S. HISTORY ERAS 1-3: PREHISTORIC AMERICA TO 1800 CE
54.	C	U.S. HISTORY ERAS 1-3: PREHISTORIC AMERICA TO 1800 CE
55.	B	WORLD HISTORY ERA 5: 300-1500 CE
56.	C	U.S. HISTORY ERA 4: 1792 TO 1861 CE
57.	C	GEOGRAPHY: RELATIONSHIP WITH HISTORY
58.	B	GEOGRAPHY: RELATIONSHIP WITH HISTORY
59.	B	WORLD HISTORY ERAS 1-3: HUMAN SOCIETY TO 4000 BCE TO 300 CE
60.	B	HISTORICAL CONCEPTS
61.	D	U.S. HISTORY ERA 5: 1850 TO 1877 CE
62.	A	U.S. HISTORY ERA 5: 1850 TO 1877 CE
63.	D	HISTORICAL CONCEPTS
64.	D	U.S. HISTORY ERAS 1-3: PREHISTORIC AMERICA TO 1800 CE
65.	A	ECONOMICS: TERMS, CONCEPTS, RELATIONSHIP WITH HISTORY
66.	C	GEOGRAPHY: RELATIONSHIP WITH HISTORY
67.	B	WORLD HISTORY ERAS 1-3: HUMAN SOCIETY TO 4000 BCE TO 300 CE
68.	C	U.S. HISTORY ERAS 1-3: PREHISTORIC AMERICA TO 1800 CE
69.	A	U.S. HISTORY ERA 4: 1792 TO 1861 CE
70.	B	HISTORICAL CONCEPTS
71.	A	U.S. HISTORY ERA 4: 1792 TO 1861 CE
72.	A	POLITICAL SCIENCE: CONCEPTS AND HISTORICAL CONNECTION
73.	B	POLITICAL SCIENCE: CONCEPTS AND HISTORICAL CONNECTION
74.	A	U.S. HISTORY ERA 4: 1792 TO 1861 CE
75.	A	U.S. HISTORY ERA 4: 1792 TO 1861 CE
76.	D	U.S. HISTORY ERA 7: 1920 TO 1945 CE

77. C ECONOMICS: TERMS, CONCEPTS, RELATIONSHIP WITH HISTORY

78. B WORLD HISTORY ERA 4: 1000-300 CE

79. B U.S. HISTORY ERA 5: 1850 TO 1877 CE

80. C U.S. HISTORY ERA 7: 1920 TO 1945 CE

81. C U.S. HISTORY ERA 5: 1850 TO 1877 CE

82. D WORLD HISTORY ERAS 1-3: HUMAN SOCIETY TO 4000 BCE TO 300 CE

83. C HISTORICAL CONCEPTS

84. A HISTORICAL CONCEPTS

85. D U.S. HISTORY ERA 9: 1970 TO THE PRESENT

86. A U.S. HISTORY ERA 5: 1850 TO 1877 CE

87. B WORLD HISTORY ERAS 1-3: HUMAN SOCIETY TO 4000 BCE TO 300 CE

88. C U.S. HISTORY ERA 5: 1850 TO 1877 CE

89. B WORLD HISTORY ERA 5: 300-1500 CE

90. A HISTORICAL CONCEPTS

91. A HISTORICAL CONCEPTS

92. A WORLD HISTORY ERA 4: 1000-300 CE

93. D WORLD HISTORY ERA 4: 1000-300 CE

94. C HISTORICAL CONCEPTS

95. C U.S. HISTORY ERA 6: 1870 TO 1920 CE

96. B U.S. HISTORY ERA 5: 1850 TO 1877 CE

97. D U.S. HISTORY ERA 5: 1850 TO 1877 CE

98. D WORLD HISTORY ERAS 1-3: HUMAN SOCIETY TO 4000 BCE TO 300 CE

99. A HISTORICAL CONCEPTS

100. C HISTORICAL CONCEPTS

www.ingramcontent.com/pod-product-compliance
Lightning Source LLC
Chambersburg PA
CBHW051425290326
41932CB00048B/3229
* 9 7 8 0 9 8 9 8 0 9 6 1 0 *